Hunt It, Clean It, Cook It, Eat It

The Complete Field-to-Table Guide to Bagging More Game, Cleaning it
Like a Pro, and Cooking Wild Game Meals Even Non-Hunters Will Love

Haley Heathman

bhc
press™

Livonia, Michigan

Edited by Hannah Ryder
Proofread by Anna Heiar

Hunt It, Clean It, Cook It, Eat It

Published by BHC Press

Library of Congress Control Number: 2020934357

ISBN: 978-1-64397-148-3 (Softcover)
ISBN: 978-1-64397-149-0 (Ebook)

For information, write:
BHC Press
885 Penniman #5505
Plymouth, MI 48170

Visit the publisher:
www.bhcpress.com

Table of Contents

Hunt It, Clean It, Cook It, Eat It

Introduction

Hey there! Thanks for grabbing my book. I'm Haley, and I'm pleased to make your acquaintance.

Now that that's out of the way, let's get to the heart of the matter: many of you have picked up this book and are intrigued. You're now flipping through the pages to see if this is the kind of book you want to buy or if you're going to put it back on the shelf and keep browsing. Perhaps you've already bought it. Or maybe you were gifted it and are now trying to figure out what you're in for.

Regardless of how it came into your possession, you're checking out the introduction because you're thinking to yourself, "This book sounds interesting, but who is this chick and why should I listen to her, of all people, when it comes to hunting and cooking wild game?"

I get it. If you're gonna drop some coin on a book and spend your valuable time on something, you want to be sure that the information in it is worthwhile, credible, and that you're going to get your money's worth, especially when the information comes from someone with zero name recognition. You're here trying to get a quick look at my credentials to see if I'm the type of person you want to learn from.

Let me be up front with you…

I'm not an expert hunter. I don't have a YouTube channel or a TV hunting show. I'm just a gal who appreciates hunting, who has connections to the hunting world, who is a keen researcher, and who wants to keep the tradition of hunting alive.

That being said, while I'm only a novice hunter, I do consider myself to be somewhat of an expert in the kitchen. In fact, that was the genesis of this book.

After spending a lot of time with hunters and sitting at many supper tables with more experienced hunters than myself—lifelong hunters, in many cases—I was more often than not left quite underwhelmed with their preparation of the wild game they cooked. Sometimes, it was barely edible and it was all I could do to choke down some of the gamey, livery meat they'd all but obliterated.

So, what *are* my credentials then?

Good question.

I grew up a Hoosier in the great state of Indiana. When I was in my twenties, I moved down to Florida to begin my career as a superyacht stewardess for the world's rich and sometimes famous. I spent ten years traveling the globe, working hand in hand with some of the world's best chefs to create elegant experiences for some of the most discerning people on the planet.

While I did not start off my yachting career as a proficient cook (growing up in Indiana, my idea of fine dining was a nice meal at Olive Garden or Red Lobster), by the end of my ten year career, I had acquired enough culinary skills to be able to feed a hungry, international crew of eight and was occasionally asked to cook for yacht owners and their guests when the regular chef was unavailable.

What a culinary journey I've had going from a humble Indiana girl who hated when her food touched on her plate to becoming someone who can expertly pair wine with food and create sumptuous meals with ingredients I had once never even heard of for the global one percent!

After I left the yachting industry, I returned to my landlubber roots and bought twenty acres in Montana complete with a gun range in the front yard. Up in rural Montana, hunting is practically a way of life. You'd be hard pressed to find someone who *didn't* hunt. I became immersed in hunting culture. My former husband was an expert hunter. I used to say, "If he kills it, I'll cook it!"

Even though my palate became exponentially more refined, I still never forgot my Indiana roots, and I felt at home with my down-to-earth Montana neighbors after having spent so many years catering to the jet-setting crowd. Nevertheless, I was quite surprised that many of the lifelong hunters I had the pleasure of becoming friends with in my post-yachting life had not mastered the art of wild game cooking.

I realized I could take my knowledge and skills and rectify this. Rather than just being mere survival gruel you plopped on a plate, I wanted to elevate wild game to something more sophisticated. I wanted to remove the stigma from wild game as something mostly inedible that only hardcore hunters liked eating and create dishes that even non-hunters would enjoy. Most importantly, I still wanted it to be approachable to your Average Joe.

I lived in a town of just a few hundred people. We did have a grocery store, but I know all too well what items and ingredients are available in a flyover country grocery store. There were no high-end grocery stores within a two-hour drive. Ingredients must be basic kitchen staples available in almost any grocery store.

I've adapted many recipes that I've cooked using non-game proteins and modified them using a similar type of wild game. Each recipe reflects any changes you'd have to make cooking wild game as compared to cooking traditional meat dishes. All recipes are my own, but some were inspired by other people I know either online or in person from my yachting days.

Not only that, but as the food sovereignty movement grows and people are more in-tune with where their food comes from and how it's raised, I decided it was crucial to not just include wild game recipes in this book, but to also give detailed instructions in how to hunt the game and the field care required.

Good-tasting meat doesn't just come from the kitchen. It starts in the field with knowing what the best species and types of game to kill are and how to treat the game in the field with the care required to be sure you're working with the highest quality specimen possible when it comes time to cook it. No amount of cooking skill will be able to salvage a poorly shot or improperly field-dressed animal.

But if I'm not a hunting expert, where did all the hunting know-how in my book come from?

Another very good question.

I'm not an expert, but I'm not an imbecile either. I've been in the field. Not only that, but I've sat around many campfires while the boys swapped stories of their most memorable hunts. That's all well and good, but those anecdotal stories merely fill out and inform the book. The real meat (pun intended) comes from the hours of interviews I did with hunting experts from across the country.

I interviewed at least a half dozen hunting guides, firearms experts, and other lifelong hunters. I spent hours upon hours asking questions about the areas of hunting that I knew I wasn't well-versed in. I have pages full of notes. I had audio interviews transcribed so that I could reference them later. Beyond that, I consulted lots of online hunting resources. I watched hours of YouTube videos and sat in front of the TV watching various hunting shows with celebrities in the hunting world.

In other words, I did my due diligence to make sure that I was only providing top-quality, well-researched, and fact-checked information. I then compiled the information and distilled it down to the best of the best tips and tricks for hunting and cleaning wild game, even coining my own names for some of the various hunting and cleaning techniques I present throughout the book.

What results is a comprehensive beginner's guide to hunting and cooking six of the most commonly hunted wild game species in North America. The information is presented in an entertaining and easy-to-read style. In other words, your eyes won't glaze over and you're not going to die of boredom when you read this book!

While this book was written with beginners in mind, there's enough information in here to appeal to hunters of all skill levels. Some hunters might be quite experienced when it comes to big game, but not waterfowl, for instance. Some hunters might consider themselves well-versed all around but will still be able to learn a few new tricks to keep up their sleeve for their next hunting season.

Or, you might be the type of hunter I had in mind when I created this book—an ace in the field but an omega in the kitchen. You will definitely get a lot out of this book.

While this book might not be a four-inch thick tome of hunting know-how written by one of the master hunters themselves, I have no doubt that you'll be both informed and entertained while reading this book. Each page packs a punch. Your time is important and I want to make sure you're getting bang for buck, not just meaningless filler.

Lastly, I want to say a few more words about why I wrote this book.

Once upon a time, I had a misconception about hunting and hunters. What astounded me the most when I was researching this book and from my experiences within the hunting world is how compassionate hunters are. Far from the barbarians many outsiders portray us as, I came to realize that the vast majority of hunters are caring individuals who are excellent stewards of the environment, contrary to popular opinion. On the hunts I've been on and at the supper table, in a touching and reverent show of appreciation, we would pray over the animal, thanking it for its sacrifice so that we could feed our families with its meat. Hunters are some of the most humane, ethical, and respectful people you'll ever come across.

Through my research, I was also surprised to discover that hunters actually pay for the majority of the conservation efforts throughout the US. Because of all this, I also was dismayed to find out that the proud hunting custom that was once as American as apple pie is slowly dying. For various reasons, both cultural and political, the days of self-reliance, tradition, and heritage are in danger.

The sport of hunting, apart from a few exceptions, has been in a steady decline since the late '80s. Each generation, fewer and fewer people are introduced to the sport. I hope and believe that we might be starting to slow the decline and the numbers might start to rise again now that food sovereignty and the importance of self-reliance are becoming popular again.

It's my hope that my book can play some small part in reigniting a passion for the sport of hunting and take the mystery out of cooking wild game meat, while reducing the stigma attached to it. I also hope that my book will inspire current hunters to get back in the field and get them excited about their next hunting season now that they're armed with all sorts of new hunting techniques and recipes to try out.

I hope you'll join me, just a humble Indiana gal who's had quite a cultural journey and awakening herself and who hopes to inspire others to save this time-honored tradition that's helped make America great throughout generations.

Happy hunting!

Haley Heathman

PART ONE
BIG GAME

Chapter One

DEER

HUNT IT

Deer Hunting—An American Love Affair

A merica's favorite game meat, good ole venison.

According to some sources, the word venison itself can be traced back to the Latin word *venus*, which was given to the Roman goddess of love.

It's only fitting that America's most hunted animal, the whitetail deer, results in venison on the table. This makes deer hunting, almost literally, an act of love.

If you're a good hunter and an ethical hunter, you'll treat the sport as such, an act of love—only taking ethical shots, always following proper safety protocols, dispensing of the animal humanely, and then using and consuming as much of the animal as possible once it's been killed.

That being said, while you might have love in your heart for the animal in a spiritual sense of the word, the real allure of deer hunting is more primal and ancestral.

Man vs. Beast. Survival. Triumph. Perseverance. Providing for family. The essence of manliness since the dawn of time.

Imagine how satisfied you feel being able to put food on the table for your family for the entire next year. Or the pride swelling within you as you watch your son or grandson take down their first buck.

Hunting is a generational sport. Hunting secrets and best practices get passed down from generation to generation. It bonds families together. It keeps alive the time-honored tradition of using the land and what God and nature provides to nourish one's own family.

But if you're one of the unfortunate ones who didn't grow up in a hunting household, how do you get started?

How do you know what kind of gun to use? What kind of ammo? Where do you go to find the deer? What do you do with it once it's been shot? How do you cook it so as to avoid the dreaded "gamey" flavor everyone has had a bad experience with?

While this book can't supplant actually getting out in the field for some real-world experience, it can give you a sound foundation from which to get started and supplement your existing knowledge.

Whether you're new to hunting or you wish to become a more complete hunter, you'll get answers to all of the above questions and more.

Before you know it, you'll learn to think of all hunting, not just deer hunting, as an act of love.

Then you, too, can pass down this tradition of love and tales of triumph to other generations to come and help preserve the heritage that has defined the essence of man since the dawn of time.

It Starts in the Off Season

Contrary to what most people think, opening day on the first week of September (for most) is not the start of deer season.

For any hunter worth his salt, deer season started in early August at the least. More than likely, it's been going on all year as you eye that buck that keeps coming around and seeing how his rack is coming in, watching where he comes from and where he goes and at what times.

No, opening day is not the start of deer season any more than the first NFL game of the year is the start of their season. They didn't just suit up for the first time since the last season during that first game.

Sure, it might be the first day of the year that counts but it only counts, and you'll only be successful in proportion to the amount of effort you put in during the off season.

So, what does it take to become a successful deer hunter?

The answers can vary depending on who you ask, but two of the most common answers are scouting and knowing your rifle.

You have to know where the deer are, first and foremost, and then you have to have confidence in your rifle skills to be able to humanely and ethically put down the deer at a comfortable distance once he comes into your sights.

The rest—tree stands, calling, decoys, etc.—is icing on the cake.

Let's take a look at what off-season tactics you should be taking to ensure in-season success.

Pound the Ground and Scan the Land

If you're new to the territory, you'll want to familiarize yourself with the lay of the land as much as possible.

This includes breaking out some topographical maps and aerial photos of where you'll be hunting.

Do you really think you can just waltz into someone else's home and win at a game of hide and seek? Of course not! That's why scouting is so important.

You'll be scanning the land and the photos looking for rivers and other water sources, fields, travel corridors, and thickets. Basically, you'll be trying to figure out where the deer are going for food, water, shelter, and the likely routes they'll be taking between each of those areas.

Even if you don't live in the area, you can still manage to complete these steps at home so you have at least some idea of where to go when you get to your hunting grounds.

If you do live in or near the area and you've done a scan of the land via map and photo, you'll want to make like a mad general and put some boots on the ground to check it out in person.

Boots on the Ground

This is when you start forming a strategy. Where will you park? How far will you have to pack in? What's the terrain like? What will you need to bring with you?

In addition to starting to get answers to these questions, you'll also be on the lookout for deer sign like tracks, droppings, rubs, and scrapes.

Finding these are obvious signs that there are deer in the area, but if you take a closer look, you can often tell *what kind* of deer are in the area.

For instance, if you see a bunch of deer tracks in some mud, take note of the size of the tracks. If there's one set that's obviously larger than the others, that means there's a mature buck in the area. You can also take a visual measure of the stride to be certain. Mature bucks will have a longer stride than yearlings and does.

Looking at the deer droppings will also give you an indication of what kinds of deer are in the area. Large clumps of deer doo-doo indicate that a large deer is in the area.

Not only that but, like most men, bucks tend to drop a deuce as soon as they leave their beds.

Large droppings near a thicket could be a strong sign that that's where the deer are bedding down. From there you just need to work out the direction they're heading for some food and water.

Less obvious signs you should be on the lookout for are scrapes and rubs. Rubs occur at the beginning of the season when bucks are rubbing the velvet off their antlers. You'll often find rubs between feeding and bedding locations.

Scrapes are made to show territorial dominance. While most common during the rut, scrapes can be found throughout the year and usually occur near food sources and in travel corridors.

By spotting these signs and marking them on the map as you're walking the land, you'll soon be able to hone in on potential zones where you can set up shop and wait for some deer.

If you're hunting public land, be mindful of the fact that other hunters are doing the same thing as you are, so be sure to have several locations scouted in case you find your spot is already taken for the day.

I like to say that when hunting on public land, you have to have a bold mentality and not be afraid to go where others haven't.

Be willing to go where other hunters won't, including the swampiest land and densest areas of the forest. This might mean packing in a bit farther from the road than most hunters are typically willing to hike.

When scouting, you'll also want to bring your binoculars and take a couple country drives so you can glass some fields. Stay at least three to four hundred yards away and keep downwind. Pay attention to which direction the deer enter the field from as that can give you an indication of where they're bedded down.

Complete these crucial pre-season scouting steps and you'll give yourself a decent shot at winning a game of hide and seek in someone else's home that can smell you coming a mile away.

The Surprising Similarities Between Rifles and Racquets

I grew up playing tennis and played tennis in college (three-time All-American and NCAA doubles runner-up my senior year, thank you very much!).

For a tennis player, you're only going to be as good as the racquet you're playing with.

Some frames are stiffer than others. There are mid-size heads, mid-plus heads, and oversize racquet heads. The grips have different lengths and widths—an NBA player would need a considerably wider grip than the one I play with.

Not to mention the string job on the racquet—what kind of string to use, how tight or how loose, should the cross strings be strung at a different poundage than the main strings…

There are all sorts of considerations to make when it comes to choosing a racquet!

How did I choose?

Well, typically at the racquet clubs I played at where I grew up in Indianapolis, they had a pro shop that sold tennis clothes, shoes, and racquets. They would often have demo racquets that you could take on the court with you during a class or a lesson to try out.

Better yet, take a couple racquets with you in case you knew right away that the first one wasn't for you.

And then you just hit like you normally would. You feel it out. You see where your ball is landing. Are you sailing them out of the court? Are you hitting a lot of mishits off the frame? Is it too heavy? Is it too light?

After a while, you begin to pick up a pattern.

For me, I noticed that the Prince racquets and the Head racquets were the most comfortable for me. Wilson racquets, despite being extremely popular and used by many top players, I never could get a feel for.

I liked the forgivingness of the Head racquets especially. I could mishit the ball and instead of it sailing three courts down, it would somehow miraculously still stay in the court or just barely miss.

I remember when I was a junior player my dad got me to try out this new innovative racquet with a weird geometric head that had some angles on the frame toward the top instead of the traditional oval-shaped head.

I played with it for a couple of months with awful results at tournaments. My family started to insist that it wasn't the right racquet for me. I resisted, thinking it was just me playing poorly and I just needed to take a few more lessons on my backhand because I kept mishitting it so badly.

Finally, my family convinced me to try another racquet.

Holy moly, amen, and hallelujah! If that didn't do the trick!

All of a sudden, I wasn't mis-hitting every other ball. I could actually sustain a rally longer than four strokes. I started winning again!

All of this is just a drawn out analogy for choosing the perfect rifle or shotgun for hunting.

That is to say that it's entirely subjective and will require some trial and error, just like choosing a tennis racquet or golf clubs. After a while, you'll begin to notice similarities and patterns.

You notice that you're way more accurate with bolt action guns than you are with pump action guns, for instance.

You also might start to become aware that although you like the lighter style guns because they're way more comfortable to carry in the field, you are way less accurate with them when it counts. So maybe something in between will work better for you.

And even though everyone swears by a Winchester .30-06, to you it just never felt like it sat right in your shoulder. That Weatherby, however—it's like you two were made for each other!

So here are a few pieces of advice to follow when choosing the right tool for the job (whether that's a rifle for deer hunting, a racquet for tennis, or a club for golf):

1. Try before you buy

This is of utmost importance. Don't buy something just because you read it was rated the best gun by such and such magazine or because your favorite TV hunter (who was paid) recommended a certain gun.

Get together with a couple of buddies and try out their guns. See if you notice a pattern about which ones feel better. Start ruling out guns by action style, make, barrel length, and weight until you finally hit the sweet spot of what you're looking for.

2. Don't throw the baby out with the bathwater!

After you've shot a certain rifle a few times and even though you like the feel of it, you notice that you're not quite as accurate with it as you want to be.

Don't hastily lament that it isn't the gun for you. It might not be the gun at all but rather the ammo! Try the same gun with different rounds of ammo in there and see if your accuracy doesn't improve before you rule out the gun entirely.

Some guns shoot as straight as a nun in a convent with one type of ammo but are as off as a piece of meat on a hot summer's day with another kind.

3. OK, it might be the gun's fault after all

For whatever reason, I didn't want to blame my racquet on my shoddy tennis performance. I thought it was me and stubbornly refused to change racquets when it was plainly obvious to everyone else that my performance suffered as soon as I switched to the new, wonky racquet head.

Sometimes, it really is the gun. If you've shot enough rounds through it, changed up the ammo, played around with the sights and the optics, and you still are constantly missing when it counts, it might be time to admit that maybe it's not the gun for you after all.

This is actually relieving as your confidence can really take a hit when you're not performing up to your expectations. Watch your confidence soar again by switching up your rifle and nailing those bullseyes from a hundred yards out like you used to do.

From Zero to Hero—Sighting in For the Win!

Have you ever stepped on a scale and been surprised at the number you saw?

You weighed two hundred pounds two weeks ago and all of a sudden you step on a scale and it's telling you you've gained five pounds, even though you know nothing's changed in the last two weeks.

What the…?

It's only then you notice that the corner of the scale got wedged underneath the corner of the bathroom counter.

You gently free it from underneath the corner it was trapped under and step back on…

Bingo! Two hundred points on the nose! You breathe a sigh of relief.

Being wedged under the bathroom vanity cupboard had put just enough pressure on the scale that when you stepped on it initially, it wasn't starting at zero but rather at five pounds. This made the final weigh-in inaccurate.

This is essentially the same thing that happens when you don't zero and sight in your rife before the start of the season. It's something that needs to be done frequently, not just once every three years.

Otherwise, it'll be like stepping on a scale that isn't calibrated properly to begin with. You've got your target in your crosshairs, but you're still missing the mark because you haven't aligned your scope with where the bullet is actually hitting.

While many hunters use the terms interchangeably, technically there is a difference between zeroing and sighting in your rifle.

Zeroing in your rifle is where an adjustable scope is re-indexed to show "0,0" for windage and elevation at your point of aim.

Sighting in describes the process whereby the point of aim (POA) is adjusted to match the point of impact (POI) at a given range. In other words, aligning the sights to match where the rifle actually impacts.

The Best Way to Sighting in Your Rifle in Three Easy Steps:

1. Bore sight your rifle

This is the preliminary step to sighting in whereby you first ensure that the barrel of your gun and the scope are both aiming at the same thing.

Put your target at twenty-five yards. Make sure your rifle is securely resting in a Lead Sled or other solid rest. Remove any ammo and, if using a bolt action, the bolt from the gun so you can see through the barrel of the gun to the target.

Can you plainly see the center of the target when you look through the barrel from behind the rifle? Good. If not, adjust the gun's position so that the target's center lines up with the bore.

From there, *without touching the gun*, adjust your optic so that the reticle is also centered on the middle of the target.

Drop down and look through the barrel of the gun again to make sure the bore is still centered. Repeat these steps as necessary until both the center of the bore and the center of the optics align.

2. Take a test shot (or group)

Once your rifle has been bore-sighted, move your target back to one hundred yards. Set your optics so that they're centered right in the middle of the bullseye.

Take a shot. You probably won't hit the bullseye. That's okay, as long as you're on paper.

If you're less experienced, you'll want to shoot a group of three shots in case the first shot is a flyer.

3. <u>Adjust your optics</u>

Do not touch or move your gun. If the gun jumped during the shot, aim your scope back to the middle of your bullseye. You should be able to see the bullet hole or group from the shot you just took visible in your scope.

With the reticle still locked on the middle of your bullseye, use the external turrets on your scope to adjust it. Move the reticle from the center of your bullseye to where your bullet hole or group average is.

As long as you didn't move your gun while you were adjusting your scope, you're all done and sighted-in!

If you take your next shot aiming right on the bullseye, you should be dead on.

So many hunters do the opposite when sighting in a rifle. That is, they start from the bullet hole and try and calculate the up/down and left/right adjustments needed to hit the bullseye instead of starting with their scope on the bullseye and just dialing in from there.

If you do it the other way, it might take you forty shots before you finally get your rifle sighted-in because you're doing a lot more guessing.

That's the sucker's way to sighting in a rifle. Good thing you're not a sucker, though, right?

What Zombies Can Teach You About Deer Hunting

Anyone familiar with zombies?

Zombies aren't smart. They're slow. They have a limited range of motion. But they do still have their senses about them. They're attracted to loud noises, bright lights, and can still sniff out humans over other zombies.

Human survivors in a zombie apocalypse use the zombie's sense of smell to their advantage by killing them and covering themselves with zombie guts. By doing this, they can literally walk through a zombie horde virtually undetected.

If you want to be a deer-killing machine, take a page from this tactic and do everything in your power to mask your luscious human scent.

While you won't have to cover yourself in deer entrails, there are other steps you'll need to take to mask your human scent before you even think about hitting the trail in search of a prize buck.

Find out how to do that below.

Smell Ya Later!

Okay, so you've done your due diligence in scouting the land and figuring out where the deer are likely to be eating and sleeping.

Your rifle is as good as gold and ready to Grim Reaper the next antlered animal that crosses your path.

Now what?

It's time to load up the truck and head out. It's game time!

The good news is, you've already done at least fifty percent of the work. If you know where the animals are (more or less) and you're an ace with your rifle, the rest of it is pretty much a waiting game.

However, you're going to be waiting an awfully long time if you don't mask your scent.

Heck, even if you're smelling shower clean, you'll still be waiting a long time before you ever lay eyes on a deer.

Not adequately masking your human scent is the #1 mistake deer hunters make that can ruin a hunt before it even begins.

Follow the six tips below and you'll be able to waltz into deer territory as easily as a fake zombie passing through a horde.

1. Before the hunt

Scent-masking begins way before you ever set foot in the field.

In the days and weeks leading up to the hunt, it means laundering your hunting clothes with a perfume-free detergent and packing them away immediately in a sealable bag or box where other human smells can't rub off.

Some people even sprinkle baking soda on their hunting clothes or pack the bag with leaves, pine needles, or other matter native to the area they'll be hunting in.

An old school trick you can do is to sit in front of a smoky campfire. Throw some wet leaves, pine needles, or damp moss on there to really smoke it up. No cooking food, however.

Take your smoky clothes off and pack them away in a sealable bag unless you're going straight out on the hunt.

2. Personal hygiene

The night before or the morning of your hunt, be sure to bathe yourself using scent-free and odor-masking soaps.

Make sure you use special scent-free deodorant as well instead of blasting yourself with scented products.

You'll even want to brush your teeth with baking soda versus your normal minty-fresh toothpaste before you head out.

And for the love of God, do not light up a cigarette the morning of your hunt. Smokers are oblivious to how bad they smell even to humans, it'll be an instant tip off to a deer whose sense of smell is a hundred plus times more powerful than that of humans.

3. Don't put on your hunting clothes until you get to your site

Scent-masking products might not be able to cover the smell of cooked breakfast, morning coffee, cigarette smoke, and the gas station if you put your clothes on at home first thing in the morning.

Put those sealable bags or boxes in your truck and don't fully suit up until you're ready to hit the trail.

4. The wind is not your friend

Deer have okay vision and very good hearing but an amazing sense of smell.

It is essential that wherever you've chosen to set up, you're *downwind* of where you expect the deer to be coming from.

On a perfect day, deer can smell you coming from half a mile away.

5. Urine luck!

It's important to realize that there is a difference between scent-blocking and scent-masking.

Scent-blocking basically erases all traces of human scent so you don't smell like anything (theoretically).

Scent-masking masks your human scent with another more natural scent that won't alarm the deer or might even attract the deer to your scent.

Popular choices are cover sprays like pine, acorn, apple, and earthy scents like cedar or sage.

You can also use urine scents like raccoon, fox, or even skunk urine.

No matter what you choose, always remember to match the hatch. That is, be sure you're using scent-maskers that are natural to the environment you'll be hunting in.

No sense in using a pine cover if you're hunting in a deciduous forest or dousing yourself and your surroundings in skunk urine if there's not a skunk to be found in the whole county.

6. Scent of a doe

Lastly there are scent attractants that you can use to lure the deer in.

One of the most popular choices is the doe in estrus scent that drives the bucks wild.

Sprinkle this around your blind or around buck scrapes to lure them into your trap.

Alternatively, you can go the "Fight Me!" route and use some buck testosterone instead. This can help lure in an angry buck that wants to defend his territory.

Assuming your human scent is properly masked, these attractants can lead a buck in by its nose into your waiting arms!

Appealing to the Other Senses to Attract a Prize Buck

We just discussed why smell is the most important sense you must be mindful of when deer-hunting.

More so than trying to attract a deer, it's more important to not repel it in the first place by smelling like a human.

Once you've got your smell under control, it's time to appeal to the other two main senses—sight and sound—to turn the final screws on that elusive buck you know is out there pining for some action.

The Four Calls of Deer Hunting

There are four main calls you can use when trying to lure in a buck. It's good to have a variety of calls on hand so you can use the right one depending on the time of the season and situation at hand.

Here's the rundown on them and how they can help:

1. <u>Grunter: the grunt call</u>

The most basic deer call of all.

It works because you can use it during all phases of the rut and is a commonly heard sound no matter what a buck is doing.

The grunt is a dominance challenge, so it's effective at arousing another buck's curiosity and getting his hackles up. He'll often come over and investigate.

It's effective for both blind calling and for when a buck is in sight but out of range and you need him to get just a few yards closer.

2. <u>Rattler: the rattle call</u>

The second most common call in a hunter's tool bag.

This sound mimics two bucks sparring. The trick is to know when to be aggressive with it.

In the pre-rut and early season, bucks are just jockeying for pecking order, not full-on fighting. So you'll want to use a light touch with your call or your antlers.

During the rut, the altercations are more furious with fights for the breeding rights for a doe in estrus. This is when you'll want to be more aggressive with your rattling.

Mix it in with some grunt calls and then sit and wait for the strategy to pay off.

3. Bleaty: the bleat call

The plaintive, helpless doe and fawn bleat.

This call is used to directly attract other does. What you're hoping to do is indirectly attract a buck that is trailing the doe.

You can use it on its own to bring in a doe with a buck on her tail that otherwise would not have come in.

You can also use it in conjunction with a grunt call to make a buck think that a hot doe in his territory is being pursued by a rival buck.

4. Wheezy: the snort wheeze call

The last resort call. This one should stay in your pocket more often than not because it's a sound that the deer themselves don't often make unless they're fighting mad.

But if you use it at precisely the right time, be ready! That buck is going to be coming in hot looking for a fight so you had better be ready to take him down once he shows.

Use the snort wheeze at the wrong time, however, and you risk scaring off a sub-dominate buck.

Learn to use these calls effectively and you can get these four dwarfs to whistle and do the work for you of calling in a mature buck.

I Spy With My Eye...

Lastly, we must make an appeal to the final sense of the deer: the eyesight.

Decoys can provide that final bit of realism to your set-up that will at long last bring in that buck that's been hanging up in the distance.

While some hunters use decoys regularly in their repertoire, many others only use decoys as a last resort late in the season when all other tactics have failed.

Suffice it to say, decoys are not a mandatory part of deer hunting but they can be an extremely effective trick to have in your bag of goodies that you can pull out when the time calls for it.

Listed below are four tried and true ways you can use decoys to seal the deal with your buck.

1. Cover your scent

As with the rest of deer hunting, covering your scent is mandatory, even with the decoy. The first thing that buck is going to do when it gets close enough is to take a whiff of what's standing in front of him. If something's not right, he'll run off faster than you can blink.

Be sure to wear gloves while handling the decoy. Once you've got it in position, spray it with an odor neutralizer.

Lastly, sprinkle a little deer scent around and underneath the decoy. Anything that will smell natural once the buck gets close enough to sniff.

2. Keep your decoy in the limelight

You want your decoy to be visible. The sooner a deer can spot your decoy, the sooner it can start heading your way to investigate. If it's too well-concealed, you risk startling the deer if it happens upon it unexpectedly.

3. <u>Heads or tails?</u>

If you're using a buck decoy, place it so the head is facing toward your blind, angling left or right. When a buck comes in, he'll almost always circle downwind of it and face it head on. This naturally puts him between you and your stand.

If it's a doe decoy, place it with the tail facing your blind. This is for the same reason. A buck is going to be more interested in the tail end of a doe and will circle behind it, giving you a closer and better shot.

4. <u>Uncle Buck or Jane Doe?</u>

One of the most important decisions to make is whether to use a buck or a doe.

If you're only going to take one decoy with you, the better choice is probably a buck. Not only that, but a subordinate buck. Some hunters have even lopped off one antler to make it look less intimidating.

A subordinate buck will tend to attract more dominant males. Using a dominant deke can scare off the subordinate bucks that are hanging around but might work wonders if you're targeting a specific alpha buck.

Using a doe and a buck together can be effective as it plays on the jealousy of the buck. He won't be too happy seeing another buck wooing Jane Doe and will want to intervene.

A solo doe can be a hit or miss proposition. On the one hand, an estrus doe can bring in that horny buck right in the middle of the rut.

On the other hand, does tend to bring in other does, which can hang around long enough to bust you. Time it right if you plan on using a solo doe.

Go Buck Wild!

You now have all the tools you'll need to be successful in the field.

From scouting the territory to readying your rifle to understanding how to appeal to a deer's senses to maximize opportunity while minimizing errors, you'll be hauling in that prize buck before you know it!

And once you do, in the next chapter I have some proven techniques for cleaning and field dressing your deer so it will be table or mount ready in no time.

From the field to the table—with love!

CLEAN IT

Field Dress Your Deer in Five Minutes or Less

Woo-hoo! You shot a deer! Time to crack open a cold one with the boys and celebrate! But don't celebrate too much—there's still important work to be done.

Good tasting game meat starts with proper field care. Especially with deer. Everyone has had a bad experience with "gamey" deer meat. Since deer is the most hunted animal in the United States, it's also the most commonly eaten game meat. If non-hunters have tried any sort of game meat, it's most likely going to be deer. And if non-hunters have had a bad experience with game meat, it's most likely going to be from deer.

This is a shame because if they have one bad experience with game meat, they're unlikely to want to try more. They'll be turned off of game meat forever and have a bad taste in their mouths —quite literally—about hunting in general.

With proper field care and cleaning, you can help prevent this.

By following the steps and best practices outlined in the coming pages, you can be an ambassador for the hunting world to non-hunters and be sure their first encounter with game meat leaves them wowed, not woozy.

Get It Clean

The number one rule of cleaning big game is to get it cooled down as quickly as possible.

Cooling it down means removing the heat-retaining guts and innards and opening up the body cavity to get air circulating in it, which gets it cooling off right away.

While it may seem like a daunting task at first, with the proper tools and a little know-how, you can have your deer cleaned and gutted in five minutes or less.

Let's go over the basic steps to field dressing your deer. Please note that every hunter does it slightly differently in terms of order of the steps. But the essential steps don't change.

Five Simple Steps to Field Dressing Your Deer in Five Minutes or Less

1. Sex organs

First thing you want to do when prepping your deer is remove the sex organs and cut around the anus.

Using your knife, cut the skin around the genitals. Once the genitals are removed, make an inverted V slit above the anus. From there, carefully cut around the anus.

You can either pull the anus out of the way slightly or tie it off with a string to prevent any poop pellets from contaminating the meat.

2. Don't bust the gut

This is the most important part. Make a very shallow incision in the skin just above where you cut the sex organs off.

Slide your fingers underneath the skin. Cut from the naval to the breastbone, keeping your fingers as a buffer between your knife and the internal organs.

You are trying to prevent yourself from puncturing the stomach and intestines.

3. He came, he sawed, he conquered

You can either keep slicing the skin all the way up to the neck or stop at the breastbone. Either way, you'll now need to cut open the rib cage.

You can use a handsaw to saw open the ribcage or you can use a larger, specialized knife that will cut through bone to open the rib cage and expose the heart and lungs.

4. Trach it 'til you make it

Reach up inside the rib cage and grab the trachea. Cut the trachea as close to the neck as possible.

Pull the trachea down towards the stomach. Cut the connective tissue holding the trachea and the entrails to the body cavity where necessary.

5. Spill your guts

Turn your deer over on its side. You should now be able to reach inside and drag out the entirety of the innards: trachea, intestines, stomach, and organs.

That wasn't so hard, was it?

Well, it is easier said than done. It will take a couple tries before you perfect your own technique, but once you get it down, you can have your deer field dressed in five minutes or less.

There are a couple other things you need to do to finish cleaning it.

You'll want to finish cleaning out any excess tissue left in the cavity, including the windpipe. It may also help to use some sticks to prop open the carcass to allow it to cool down even more.

If you have time, you can hang the deer by the antlers in a tree for twenty minutes or so to let any remaining blood drain out of the body before you load it up and take it home. Otherwise, you can leave the head propped up on a log or rock to allow the blood to drain down the incline.

It's not recommended that you rinse the inside with water unless you have punctured the stomach or intestines or gut shot the deer. Water can promote bacteria growth.

And ta-da! You're ready to show off your bad boy to your friends and take it to be processed (or start processing it yourself).

Not All Heroes Wear Capes, But Trophy Bucks Do!

It's seven a.m., damp, and chilly as you're silently sitting in your blind just settling in for the long haul of what you assume will be a full day of hunting. The field glistens with dew as a light fog hangs over the valley. The sun is just peeking out above the horizon, casting a majestic haze as the light starts illuminating some of the misty water particles hanging in the air. More out of boredom than anything else, you throw out a soft grunt call, not really expecting anything in return so early in the morning given the misty conditions.

A minute goes by. Your mind starts to wander a bit. Did I remember to put the rain jacket in the truck? Hungry already, should have eaten more for breakfast. If I don't get anything today, I might try that pasture near the Allen ranch tomorrow. Should probably get some new boots, these are getting worn out...

Then you hear it. Your ears perk up. The hair on the back of your neck stands up.

You slowly turn head in the direction of the noise. What was that? Leaves rustling? Or did I just imagine it?

Your eyes strain to see through the fog. A ray of sunshine reaches a long finger through the haze as if to part through it like a curtain and there you see it...

Your heart almost stops in your chest.

You see the rack first. A perfect symmetrical eight-point rack. Not ten points, but the thing is wide and thick. Your eye is drawn down to the neck. It's so thick, a pro wrestler would be jealous.

Can this be happening?

One hundred yards out...usually not a problem, but in this haze you want another twenty yards just to be certain.

You throw out another call. This seems to agitate the buck a bit, and he moves a few steps closer.

Better, but not quite enough. You seem to be at an impasse as he hangs off in the distance for several minutes.

You decide to throw a rattle at him to see if that gets him any closer.

Bingo! His territorial instinct gets the better of him, and he decides he needs to come closer to investigate.

You raise your gun waiting for the buck to turn broadside as he takes long, confident strides in your direction.

As if on cue, the sun breaks over the horizon and sets the valley aglow in its warm illuminating light. The buck pauses and turns his head around ever so slightly as if wondering where this light came from.

This is it! You have your shot! Your heart pounding out of your chest you exhale half a breath and…boom!

You see the buck take the impact as it reflexively starts off. You know it was a bullseye as you watch it start to falter in the distance.

Adrenaline pumping through your veins, you give the buck several moments to expire before you go after him, but you already know this one is going to be hanging prominently in your trophy room.

My Taxidermist Told Me So

What seems like an eternity later, you finally leave your blind and set off to track him. It's no hard task as he only managed to make it another fifty yards before finally succumbing to his wound. You say a quick prayer over the impressive animal thanking him for his sacrifice so that you can feed your family.

Knowing you want this to be a trophy animal, you set about gutting the deer the way your taxidermist told you.

You only cut the skin as far up as the breastbone so as to leave the entire chest area undisturbed. Rather than sawing open the breastbone, you have to reach up through it to get to the windpipe and trachea and dislodge that. The rest is business as usual…

You finally get the animal back to your place and hung up from the hind legs. Time for the real work to begin.

You recall the steps your taxidermist taught you about how to properly cape a deer for a shoulder mount.

First, you make a cut completely around the body of the deer at the rear of the breastbone where you stopped your incision as you were gutting the deer. This leaves your taxidermist plenty of skin to work with for whatever kind of shoulder mount you want.

You then start on the front legs. Beginning in between the knee and the elbow of the leg, you make a circular incision around the width of the leg. From there, you start your vertical cut just along the line of where the brown fur meets the white fur on the inside of the leg.

You carry on up to the armpit area very carefully following that line where brown meets white. Where the line of white fur stops at the armpit, you then make a straight line up the torso to intersect with the first cut around the body that you made.

This is where it gets tedious. Crank up your favorite song for this part so at least you can keep your toes tapping and head bobbing along while you carefully skin the animal.

Be sure to roll the skin away from the carcass as you're skinning it to avoid getting hair on the meat.

The rest of the skinning isn't hard, it just takes some time to carefully remove the skin from the meat without cutting the skin or butchering the meat in the process.

Eventually, you get to the point to where the skin is as removed as it can be and is dangling inside out over the head and the antlers like a t-shirt that got stuck on the baseball cap on your head as you were removing it.

Now, it's time to take the head off.

After a brief moment of indecision, the lightbulb goes off in your head when you recall your taxidermist telling you that it's best to remove the head four inches below the base of the skull. With three to four inches of neck muscle, he has enough to measure so that he can get the proper mannequin for the mount. You don't need any more than that— three or four inches will do the trick.

You grab your knife and start cutting around the neck muscle four inches from the back of the skull until you hit the vertebra. Now all that's left to do is grab your electric saw and saw through the neck bone to completely remove the head from the body.

Phew! Done!

You take a swig of your beer and wipe off your brow as you admire your work.

It was a hard day's work, but nothing beats the feeling of knowing that hard work has resulted in food on the table for your family and a trophy animal to adorn your walls at home.

You can't wait to stand under your mount and tell the story of the majestic buck in the misty meadow for decades to come.

Now Let's Eat!

You have the trophy on your wall to brag about for years to come, now it's time to put some food on the table that all your friends will be raving about for weeks.

Next, we'll get into all of the delicious ways to prepare and cook your venison and avoid the dreaded "gamey" flavor that turns so many people off of game meat for good.

By following the proper steps to field care that you learned in this chapter, you're already well on your way to amazing, mild-tasting venison good enough to fool your friends into thinking they're eating beef—until you spill the beans after the meal!

COOK IT

Deer Recipes That Will Make Your Mouth Water

When most non-hunters think of game meat, most often they probably think of deer. Similarly, if someone has had a bad experience with game meat, it's probably because of deer.

Why is that?

There are several reasons why that could be:

- Wrong type of deer
- Not a clean kill
- Not processed properly
- Poor cooking preparation

There could be a variety of other reasons as well, but these are the most common. While I can't do anything about whether someone shot the oldest, most haggard buck of the bunch, I can see to it that, no matter what, they prepare it properly.

Axis of Deer Eating

Believe it or not, not all deer are created equal when it comes to how it tastes. Whitetail deer is probably the most common deer to shoot and eat, but is it the tastiest? Well, that's debatable. There's a case to be made that Axis deer, found almost exclusively in Texas and Hawaii, produces the best venison.

Mule deer is widely known not to be the best eating because they feed on bitter conifers and sage grass that makes the meat taste extra gamey. The best mule deer is probably only as good as an okay whitetail (generally speaking). If you fell prey to any of the above taste-killers, forget about it.

While whitetail might not be the absolute best, it's pretty darn good. Plus, given its widespread availability throughout pretty much every region of the United States, it's the easiest one to put on the table no matter where you are.

For simplification purposes, the recipes in this section are tailored to whitetail deer. They will probably work with any other type of deer, but not guaranteed.

Fat Is Phat, Yo

Let's chat about fat, shall we? Whether you process the deer yourself or take it to someone else to process it, you can't forget the fat!

Game meat is extremely lean. What little fat a deer has on it isn't very tasty and needs to be trimmed off before processing, leaving you with just the meat.

If you try and grind up just the meat without adding any fat back into the mixture, you're going to wind up with a dry, crumbly mess that's going to taste like fake meat-like morsels.

When you go to process your venison, it's common to add some beef or pork fat back into the mixture. This gives it both fat and flavor, ensuring a juicy, moldable, and delicious bit of meat.

For us, when we do ground venison, we do an 85/15 mixture of venison to beef fat. You can get away with 90/10, but I wouldn't recommend going any lower than that. If you're processing it yourself, some people just go ahead and mix the venison with some bacon. Bacon makes everything better after all, right?

Most people turn some of the lesser cuts into snack sticks or sausages. For sausages, I like to use pork fat. You can go all the way and do a bratwurst style sausage. A common one to make is a jalapeño-cheddar sausage. These can be sliced up and used to flavor all sorts of things from a crab boil to shrimp and grits to a variety of soups and more.

No matter what, just remember that fat equals flavor. Don't be afraid to use it when processing your meat whether it's in the form of beef or pork fat, bacon, or cheese. All of it will go a long way to make sure you're starting off on the right foot when cooking your game.

Venison Is the New Beef for Dinner

The best thing about venison is that you can treat it almost exactly like you would beef. Especially anything that you would have used ground beef in, you can almost always substitute ground venison for: spaghetti Bolognese, lasagna with meat sauce, meatloaf, tacos, sloppy joes, nachos—you name it. There's no need to re-invent the wheel when it comes to ground venison.

While these are the recipes I use when cooking with venison, you can certainly use your own favorite recipes and substitute venison in wherever you would typically use ground beef.

Venison Meatloaf

- 2 eggs
- 1 celery stalk, diced
- 1 carrot, diced
- 1 8-oz. can of tomato sauce
- 1 medium onion, chopped
- 1 cup dry bread crumbs
- 1 tsp. salt
- 1/4 tsp. pepper

- 1 - 2 pounds ground venison
- 2 tbsp. brown sugar
- 2 tbsp. brown or dijon mustard
- 2 tbsp. white vinegar

Instructions:

1. Preheat oven to 350 degrees.

2. In a large bowl, lightly beat the eggs.

3. Add tomato sauce, veggies, bread crumbs, salt, pepper and venison to the bowl. Using your hands, mix until all ingredients are just combined. Do not over mix.

4. Press mixture into an ungreased 9" x 5" loaf pan.

5. Combine brown sugar, mustard, and vinegar and pour over the meat loaf.

6. Bake uncovered for approximately 70 minutes or until a thermometer reads 165 degrees.

My friends go crazy for this recipe. The brown sugar/mustard/vinegar mixture on the top along with the tomato sauce in the loaf itself gives it a slight BBQ flavor and produces a moist and flavorful meatloaf.

Normally, meatloaf goes well with mashed potatoes and gravy, but given the slightly sweet BBQ flavor this loaf has, I like to do a couple of baked sweet potatoes to go with it.

If you wrap them in cling wrap and put them in the microwave, they'll be done in 6-8 minutes. Otherwise, you can poke some holes in them, wrap them in foil, and bake the potatoes along with the meatloaf. Start checking on the potatoes after about 45 minutes. Once they're soft to the touch or a knife inserts easily into them, they're done.

Venison Chili

- 1 tbsp. olive oil
- 2 medium onions, chopped
- 3 garlic cloves, chopped
- 1 tsp. dried oregano
- 2 tbsp. chili powder, divided
- 1 tsp. ground cumin
- Salt and pepper to taste
- 1 pound ground venison or venison stew chunks
- 1 28-oz. can diced or crushed tomatoes
- 1 12-oz. bottle dark beer
- 3/4 cup chicken or beef stock
- 1 15-oz. can kidney or chili beans, drained

Instructions:

1. Heat oil in a large sauce pan over medium high heat.

2. Add onions and sauté until tender, around 4 minutes. Add garlic and cook until softened, 1-2 minutes.

3. Stir in oregano, 1 tbsp. chili powder, cumin, salt and pepper. Add in venison and cook until brown on all sides.

4. Stir in tomatoes and remaining chili powder into the mix. Add beer and broth. Bring to a simmer and cook uncovered 1-2 hours, stirring occasionally.

5. Just before serving, stir in beans. Taste and adjust seasonings as needed.

This is one of the best venison chili recipes I've come across. You can play with spices a bit. One recipe I saw called for a can of chipotle peppers in adobo sauce if you like a spicy chili, or you can just add in a pinch of cayenne pepper.

This recipe is very versatile as well. You can serve it as is, top it with some sour cream and shredded cheese, or use it to top a baked potato, rice, or bowl of pasta.

If you really want to go all out, you can make some cast iron jalapeño-cheddar corn bread to go with it, and then you'll think you done died and went to heaven!

No matter the season, this chili is sure to be a winner!

Venison, Sausage, and Lentil Soup

- 3 tbsp. butter
- 1 pound ground venison or venison stew chunks
- 1 pound venison sausage (or other mild link sausage)
- 1 white or yellow onion, chopped
- 3 carrots, chopped
- 2 garlic cloves, chopped
- 1 tsp. dried thyme
- Salt and pepper to taste
- 1/2 tsp. ground cumin
- 1 pound of lentils
- 2 cups of water
- 3 cups beef or chicken broth

Instructions:

1. Heat butter in a large stockpot over medium heat. Brown venison and sausage in batches and remove from pan with slotted spoon.

2. Sauté onions and carrots in pot for 4-5 minutes. Add garlic and sauté for 1 minute more.

3. Add thyme, salt and pepper, cumin, lentils, water and beef broth. Add venison and sausage back to stew pot and bring to a boil. Once it reaches a boil, turn to low and simmer for an hour, stirring occasionally. If soup becomes too dry, add extra water throughout the process.

Now this recipe might not seem like much, but I'm telling you it is delicious! The beauty of this recipe is its simplicity. It's not trying to impress you with a dozen random ingredients and flavors. There are just a few staple, everyday ingredients and yet somehow they combine to form one big bowl of deliciousness.

This recipe is screaming to be served with a nice, crusty piece of sourdough bread slathered in butter. I dare you to stop eating it!

Baby Got Backstrap

Now that I've shared various ways to cook up your ground venison, it's time to talk about that "pièce de résistance" (said in your best French accent): the venison backstrap.

It's the filet mignon of venison. The piece you just go ahead and take off right then and there and cook up while the rest of the carcass is hanging because you can't wait to get that tender piece of fresh, wild game meat in your mouth.

This is the one you don't want to get wrong. I'm going to say it pretty much every chapter for every type of game meat, but this is the piece you don't want to overcook.

Rule #1 of cooking game meat: Do not overcook it.

Rule #2 of cooking game meat: Don't forget rule #1.

My definition of overcooked is anything above a medium. Medium is borderline. You might just get away with it.

Ideally, you'll want to shoot for medium-rare: *a warm, red center*. A rare piece of meat will have a cool, red center. A medium piece of meat will have a hot pink center.

You want that center to be red, not pink, if at all possible. And if there's no red or pink in there at all…well, you better make sure you've got a lot of dipping sauce to go with that loin! You're going to need it to mask the gamey flavor and help chew and swallow the piece of leather you just cooked.

All those people out there who claim that game meat tastes too gamey probably said that after having a piece of overcooked, dry, rubbery venison that tasted like a cross between liver and rotten eggs.

I used to classify myself as someone who didn't much care for venison. I'd eat elk all day long, but all I could taste when it came to venison was that earthy, livery taste that only true outdoorsman love.

That taste comes from either the deer itself, which sometimes can't be helped, or from the poor preparation of the meat. When cooked correctly, you can really minimize that well-known, gamey taste of venison and turn it into a meal that everyone will enjoy.

It's worth noting that with all these recipes, you can use either backstrap or tenderloin. You'll have to reduce the cooking time on the tenderloin because it's a thinner, smaller piece of meat than the backstrap.

Internet forums and websites may tell you to go ahead and slice up your tenderloin or loin into medallions and cook them up that way. I don't recommend that.

When done that way, it's nearly impossible to get the loin to a perfect medium-rare. With such thin slices, you almost can't help but overcook your meat. If you do it this way, you're almost ensured that you'll violate Rule # 1 of cooking game meat.

If you leave the loin intact, you can get a brown crust on the outside, which gives it a nice flavor (think like when you're searing a steak, how delicious is that crisp outside?). Plus, you significantly minimize the risk that you'll over cook the loin.

My advice: sear it and cook it first, slice it and serve it second.

Grilled Venison Loin with Horseradish Cream Sauce

- 1 1/2 -2 pounds venison loin
- Salt and pepper
- 1 1/2 tbsp. mixed dry herbs like rosemary, thyme, and oregano
- 3 tbsp. olive oil
- 1 cup sour cream
- 2 tbsp. grated horseradish
- 2 tsp. chopped fresh parsley or chives
- Juice and zest of 1 lemon

Instructions:

1. Season the meat with salt and pepper.

2. In a small bowl, mix the herbs with the olive oil and spread evenly over the meat. Refrigerate for at least 2 hours. Take meat out of refrigerator at least 30 minutes before cooking to bring it up to room temperature.

3. Heat your grill or your skillet to medium-high heat. Grill meat on one side without moving it for 4-5 minutes. Flip and cook 4-5 minutes more until evenly browned on all sides. Do not over cook. Meat should be nicely browned on the outside but nice and red on the inside. Poke the meat with your tongs. If there's still some give to it like the fleshy part of your palm, it's perfect! If it feels hard, get that sucker off the grill ASAP!

4. Loosely cover and let rest for 10 minutes. The meat will still rise in temperature while it's resting and finish the cooking process, so don't be scared it's not cooked enough. If in doubt, always use your meat thermometer to be sure.

5. Mix the sour cream, horseradish, fresh herbs, lemon juice and zest in a small bowl. Season with a pinch of salt. Serve the sauce on the side or dollop on top of the venison loin.

This recipe treats the loin almost as you would a nice prime rib with a tangy horseradish sauce to complement the tender rare to medium-rare meat.

I've learned that game meat, particularly venison, which is more prone to have that bitter, livery taste to it than elk, needs a fruity or zippy sort of sauce to counterbalance that earthy taste of the meat.

Brown gravies and mushroom sauces don't go as well on venison as they do on a beef cube steak, for instance. There's not enough sweetness or acidity to cut through the gamey meat. The thickness and earthiness of brown gravies only serve to make the gaminess of the venison even more pronounced rather than balancing out that taste. A fruit sauce like the one below will be a winner with whatever kind of big game meat you're cooking.

Roasted Venison Backstrap With Red Currant Sauce

- 1 1/2 - 2 pounds venison loin
- 1/2 cup Port wine
- 3 (3-inch) strips of orange peel
- 1/2 tsp. black pepper
- 1/4 tsp. ground all spice
- 1 bay leaf
- 1 sprig fresh thyme
- Salt and pepper
- 2 tbsp. olive oil
- 1/4 cup cold butter, divided
- 1 tbsp. minced shallots
- 1 clove minced garlic
- 1/4 cup sugar
- 1/2 tsp. ground cinnamon (or 1 cinnamon stick)
- 1/2 cup demi-glace*
- 1 1/2 cups red currants **

*If you don't have demi-glace, take 1 cup of beef stock plus 1/4 cup of red wine or cooking sherry (or just beef stock if you don't have either) and reduce it down to 1/2 cup of liquid. This produces a thicker, more concentrated flavor similar to a demi-glace.

** If you don't have fresh red currants, you can use an equivalent amount of fresh blueberries instead or 1/4 cup of red currant jelly.

Instructions:

1. Place venison in a sealable bag or a non-reactive container. Combine Port wine, orange peel, pepper, allspice, bay leaf, and thyme and pour over venison. Seal and refrigerate minimum 4 hours to overnight.

2. Preheat oven to 400 degrees.

3. Remove venison from marinade, reserving marinade.

4. Season all sides of loin with salt and pepper.

5. Heat olive oil in a large, oven proof skillet over high heat. Sear the loin on all sides briefly, 1-2 minutes or just long enough to get a nice brown crust on the loin.

6. Place skillet in the oven and roast for 17-20 minutes or until a thermometer in meat reaches 125 degrees. Do not overcook.

7. Remove loin from pan and let rest for 10 minutes. Do not wash pan.

8. Add 1 tbsp. of butter to the skillet used to cook the venison. Heat over medium-high heat. Add the shallots and garlic and cook for 30 seconds.

9. Add reserved marinade, sugar, and cinnamon to the mixture. Bring to boil and cook until the mixture is reduced by half, around 3-4 minutes. The sauce should be thick and syrupy.

10. Add demi-glace and currants and bring to a low simmer. Cook until currants are softened and sauce coats the back of a spoon, 5-7 minutes.

11. Remove orange peel, cinnamon stick, and bay leaf from sauce. Adjust seasonings with salt and pepper.

12. Remove sauce from heat and stir in remaining butter. Serve over sliced venison loin.

How good does this sound?

Backstrap can be cooked simply and deliciously with just some salt and pepper and some oil, or maybe your favorite dipping sauce. Some nights you just want to get fancy. If you ever want to impress some dinner guests and show them how truly elegant and refined game meat can be, this is the recipe to use.

I know some of these ingredients are a bit fancier and harder to come by than the ingredients used in most of the other recipes in this book, but if you're an experienced cook, you should be able to make appropriate substitutions where needed if some of the ingredients aren't available to you.

If you serve this over some wild grains or wild rice pilaf and fresh green beans, you are going to have one truly gorgeous and impressive plate sure to impress your friends.

Don't Fear the Deer

When I say fear, I don't mean literally be scared of a deer. If you're scared of a deer, whether shooting or cooking it, hunting probably isn't your sport anyway!

What I mean is don't be afraid to experiment and try new ways to cook and elevate your venison. Sure, ground venison isn't really anything special. But even that can be ruined if you don't take proper care of your meat both before and during your cooking it.

Processing your meat properly is the first step to ensuring you can make a tasty meal out of it. Don't think that it's "just" venison so there's no need to do anything special with it. If you don't process it properly, it's not going to taste good no matter what you do with it .

A deer that's been well handled and cared for throughout the whole field to table process can be mighty tasty. If you don't honor that entire process, your meat is going to taste anywhere from underwhelming to downright disgusting.

And believe me, if someone has a bad experience with venison, it could tarnish their whole perspective on game meat for years to come.

So don't fear the deer. Don't be afraid to take your venison cooking game to the next level and proudly show off to your friends how delicious game meat can be when you properly take care of your animal from start to finish in the whole, beautiful field to table process.

Chapter Two

ELK

HUNT IT

Elk Hunting—Prepare for Battle

A number of hunters were asked a question one day: Why are you an elk hunter?

Sure, all hunting is special and gratifying in its own way. But what is it about elk hunting that keeps you coming back year after year given the arduous nature of the task at hand and the relatively low success rate?

The responses varied from person to person, but most of them could be boiled down to the following:

- "I love being in the great outdoors."

- "For the premium table fare…quite possibly the best game meat out there…"

- "I love living life at my own pace."

- "The challenge is formidable."

- "The camaraderie in elk camp is like a band of brothers."

- "No rigors of work and home responsibilities. Just the evening ritual of preparing for and anticipating the next day's hunt."

- "Being in my best shape of the calendar year."

- "I want a great trophy, preferably bigger than yours!"

In some ways, DIY elk hunting can be likened to going through boot camp—it's agonizing, tedious, physically grueling, and mentally challenging. But at the same time, there's an odd comfort in the routine, you learn to relish the discomfort, and the bonds formed with your hunting buddies when you're 8,000 feet up a mountain and need to rely on each other for survival in the wilderness are similar to the bonds formed when you're in the service and need to rely on the cohesiveness of your unit to survive an encounter with the enemy.

The stakes might not be quite as high when elk hunting, but the emotions are just as real.

Approaching your elk hunt with a similar mindset as you would take preparing for battle will go a long way toward ensuring success.

For instance, you need to be in top physical shape, consult maps and images to familiarize yourself with the territory your prey is hiding in, keep your weaponry honed in and deadly, and have a battle plan going into the hunt.

Let's take a closer look at what all this means and how having a battle-front mentality can increase your odds of filling your elk tag.

Sweat Now or Bleed Later

This is a common refrain given during basic training to new recruits. Essentially, it means that you need to put in the hard work now getting in shape and turning your body into a machine that will go the distance, or pay the price later.

People often underestimate the amount of drudgery and physical exertion that is required to hunt elk.

There are a number of factors at play that you often don't have to deal with when hunting other types of game. These include, but are not limited to, the following:

Altitude

Elk spend most of the year at altitudes above 7,000 feet, often as high as 11,000 feet. Oxygen is thinner, breathing is harder, and dehydration is quicker at those elevations. Altitude sickness is a real thing and is something one must acclimatize to gradually if you don't live at that elevation.

Weather

Weather is particularly unpredictable at altitude as well. You can go from 70 and sunny to heavy snow within just a matter of hours.

Terrain

As if the altitude wasn't enough, elk, especially trophy bulls, tend to live in some of the gnarliest terrain possible—over ridges and down canyons. There's a lot of hiking up and down steep slopes and through thick brush and timber.

Distance

Elk are huge animals that cover a lot of ground, much more than deer and other small game. Plan on hiking at least five miles per day through steep and gnarly terrain in less-than-ideal weather conditions.

These are all the things you'll be contending with just to get within shooting distance of an elk...and if you actually end up shooting one, your work just tripled!

All of this is to say that if you want to be a successful elk hunter, you need to spend at least a month or two before the season even starts getting in shape. If you're not in shape physically, you won't be able to go the distance—quite literally—to go where the elk are.

Sure, you hear elk tales about people who happen upon a bull on day one just a mile from where they left their ATV, but don't count on it!

If you're ready to sweat now so you don't have to pay later (in the form of blistered feet, missed opportunities, and a bruised ego) check out the following pre-season workout tips.

Six Pre-hunt Exercises You Need to be Doing NOW in Order to be Elk Fit for Season

Treadmill/Stair Climber Training

If you don't have the luxury of living in the mountains, you need to start training as if you are. This means utilizing the elevation setting on your treadmill and jumping on the stair climber machine so you can put in some time sweatin'.

It's important when using these machines to rely as little as possible on the handlebars—you won't have that luxury in the field so don't train like it at home.

Hike

If you live within range of some rugged territory, nothing will beat getting out in nature and hoofing it. Start with some easy, light hikes. Once those are comfortable, start adding in some challenges and realism.

Increase the amount of time. Start wearing your pack. Increase the amount of weight in your pack until you're able to carry forty pounds on your back comfortably for hours. Wear the same boots you'll be wearing in the field to make sure they're properly broken in.

Get off the beaten track

If you've done all of the above, it's time to find a place where you can safely get off the beaten track. There are no manicured trails in elk hunting. You'll be bushwhacking your way to your bull elk and need to be ready to fight your way through felled timber, thick brush, and rocky slopes. Put on your hiking boots, fill up your pack, and get ready to spend a day getting uncomfortable.

This is important for breaking your gear in as well. Boots that feel comfy walking on flat land might start rubbing you the wrong way once you start having to climb an incline or steady yourself down a slope. Better to find out now—and break them in or find a new pair—than on day two of a five day hunt!

Carry your kid

If you don't have any space to hike or use a treadmill, you'll have to improvise. If there aren't any trails to follow, put your kid or grandkid in one of those backpack carriers and give them the ultimate piggyback ride around the block a few times. This will get you used to carrying around an extra twenty or thirty pounds on your back, and your kid will love being able to spend some time with you for a while.

Run some bleachers

This is another option for those who don't have the luxury of living within driving distance of a nice trailhead. We all live within driving distance of some bleachers, however, usually as close as our nearest high school.

During the summer months, you'll more than likely have the stadium to yourself and can wake up early in the morning for several rounds of bleacher training. Alternate between light and fast sessions where you're working on your cardio to more endurance and strength-based training where you fill your pack up, strap it on your back, and walk at a gradual pace for an hour or more up and down the stairs.

Strength training

You can't be fit for an elk hunt without incorporating some strength training into your regime. This could mean anything from kettle bell lifting to weight training at the gym to resistance training using your body weight doing pushups, planks, and lunges.

Strengthening your legs is going to be the priority since hiking is going to be the bulk of the physical exertion. Chest and arms is next so you'll be able to draw your bow and hold draw, plus field dress and quarter your elk.

Core exercises also shouldn't be forgotten since a strong core results in a strong back so you're better able to carry a heavy pack.

The routine itself isn't as important as the fact that you're just out there getting yourself fit and ready for elk season. This will be the base upon which all other elements rest when it comes to a successful elk hunt.

Recon Like a Marine So You'll Be Swift, Silent, and Deadly in the Field

Recon—a.k.a. scouting—is of paramount importance no matter what kind of hunting you do but is especially important when it comes to elk hunting.

Without proper scouting, your five-day elk hunt may turn into just a five-day nature walk with nary a sighting of an elk.

The principal mission of Marine Force Recon is to observe, identify, and report any enemy activity.

These are often stealth missions beyond the reaches of artillery or naval gunfire support. Hence their motto, "Swift, silent, deadly." If a single round is fired, they consider their mission a failure.

The mission of Recon Marines is not to engage the enemy but merely to collect intelligence on the enemy for use in future battle.

This is your same mission when you go about scouting in anticipation of elk hunting season. Obviously you won't be shooting at anything, you're just gathering signs of elk activity, movements, and probable locations where elk will be hiding so you can formulate a game plan come elk season.

There are two primary ways of doing elk recon: pound paper and pound ground. While it's best to use both methods in order to maximize your scouting and recon intelligence, doing one or the other is better than doing nothing at all.

As the saying goes, "Failing to plan is planning to fail!"

If you do no elk scouting at all, you might as well plan on going on an extended backcountry hiking and camping trip as your chances of blindly finding an elk are slim to none!

Seven Swift and Silent Scouting Tactics to Ensure Deadly Results Come Hunting Season

1. Narrow it down

As soon as you know what Game Management Unit (GMU) you'll be hunting, you'll need to start focusing in on probable elk locations. Take into consideration which season you'll be hunting (bow, rifle, late) and start pinpointing areas where elk are likely to be during that season.

Given that each GMU can be as large as 200 to 1,000 square miles, you'll want to narrow your focus down to a couple of areas about six to eight square miles each.

2. Map it out

Invest in a recent U.S. Forest Service and/or Bureau of Land Management (BLM) topographic map series. This is especially important if you don't live in the region in which you'll be hunting. Studying these maps will be invaluable.

These maps show important info like drainage patterns, elevations, roads, trails, and land status.

Land status is important as you'll be able to see which lands are private, park lands, and any travel restrictions (foot, horseback, motorized vehicles).

Hone in on good potential areas at least two miles away from motorized trails since that's where elk are more likely to be.

3. Locate elk magnets

Real talk: elk require four main things to survive—food, water, cover, and space. Looking at your maps, aerial photos, and Google Earth images, you should identify where elk will be going for these four main things during the season you'll be hunting them.

While it's still warm out, elk will be eating green grasses at higher elevations. As it cools, the elk will descend and start feeding on woody plants and shrubs.

Finding watering holes is a great strategy in early seasons when elk congregate near wallows. Later in the season it won't be as fruitful once the elk have felt a bit of hunting pressure near such areas.

Locating cover is important as well. This is where you'll be most likely to bust a bull bedding down. Elk bed down in thick timber or oak brush scrub lands. The larger the patch of cover, the more the elk like it.

Lastly, elk need space for their herd to spread out, roam, and feed. Look for likely travel corridors between where the elk will be bedding down and where they'll be feeding, keeping in mind that elk tend to keep moving instead of visiting the same spot every day like deer do.

4. Pound ground!

Once you've identified several areas with potential, it's time to put some boots on the ground.

It's important to remember that, in pre-season scouting, you're not necessarily looking for where the elk are at that moment because they're unlikely to still be there come hunting season.

You'll be looking for signs that elk have used an area previously and is one they're likely to come back to.

Look for things like partially dead aspens or pines, stressed shrubs, and dead grass that has ends clipped off like a lawn mower. If you're finding antler sheds, you may be looking too low.

5. Timber!

From your maps, you should have identified nice dense patches of timber that are likely places for cover. You should also be looking for thinned out patches of timber due to fires or thinning operations. Elk especially love burnt timber because of the new grasses that grow afterward.

Thinned out timber is ideal because the elk feel comfortable and safe but are easily spotted by hunters. Thinner timber make for better shooting lanes and clearer shots.

Keep looking for old sign in the timber forests such as old droppings and heavily browsed shrubs.

6. Glass on

Searching for elk sign is useful, but ideally when scouting you want to see actual elk. This is when glassing helps.

Find a high point with plenty of 360 degree visibility. Bring a high-quality set of binoculars and a spotting scope to scan the surrounding lands for elk herds with lots of mature bulls.

If you're only seeing a few solitary bulls, it might be worth driving to another spot to glass from to locate a denser population of elk. It might be more beneficial to locate the cows because that's where the bulls will be headed come September for the rut.

Look for potential feeding meadows at dawn and dusk and, more importantly, if the elk are feeding and possibly even returning there.

See if you can locate saddles, north slopes, basins, benches, and pinch points that might not have been readily visible on your maps and make sure to mark them down or note the GPS coordinates.

7. <u>Smile, you're on camera!</u>

One final tactic you can use in your pre-hunt scouting regimen is setting up trail cams in the area you'll be hunting.

Trail cams are extremely effective for patterning elk behavior, especially if you have the luxury of doing it year after year. For instance, you might learn that the last week in August is the prime time to hunt a certain watering hole because after that, the bulls leave the area.

Set your trail cams in some of the transition, feed, and cover areas you've pinpointed from map scouting or ground scouting. Wallows are particularly good places to set up cameras.

Check your cameras every two to four weeks. You'll get a good idea of whether or when elk are passing through the area, how many head, and the size of any bull elk traveling with the herd. You can adjust your strategy based on what you see—or don't see—on your camera.

Knowing and familiarizing yourself with the territory you'll be hunting as much as possible in advance will exponentially increase your odds of walking out with your tag filled.

You wouldn't enter enemy territory without knowing in advance where they're likely to be hiding, possible escape routes, supply lines, and so forth. Not knowing this intel would be a recipe for disaster.

Same can be said for elk hunting. Follow the above scouting tips, and you'll be well on your way to executing a successful mission.

Elk Hunting Battle Plans and Strategies That Work

Now that your scouting is complete and season has arrived, it's time to put a strategy in place.

By this time, you should have pinpointed at least a few areas with potential that you want to hunt first.

Important considerations now need to be made.

• How many days do you have to hunt?

• Where will you be setting up camp?

• Where is the nearest road or trail?

• How far are you going to need to hike in?

• Will you be returning to elk camp every night or primitive camping as you go along?

• What season will you be hunting?

• Will you be hunting alone or with a buddy?

Once you start answering these important questions, you can start formulating a plan for how you want to approach your hunting season.

Strategies will vary depending on the answers to the above questions, plus all the other myriad considerations that must be made come elk hunting season.

While every hunt will be different and even the best laid plans can be foiled by a world-wary, mature elk who's seen enough hunting seasons to know better, one must always have a plan in mind and the knowledge to be able to adapt and change plans depending on the circumstances.

With the help of the strategies and tips outlined below, you'll greatly increase your chances of becoming one of the only twenty percent of hunters who walk out with their elk tags filled in a year.

Call Me!

There is a very delicate song and dance required to call in a big bull, hoping maybe he will respond to it.

The operative word in this whole strategy is "maybe."

As in, "should I even be calling right now?" Maybe.

Or "will he even answer me back?" Maybe.

Lifelong elk hunters will tell you that elk calling has been less effective over the years because the elk have been less vocal.

Mature bull elk especially have heard it all before and are almost immune to all but the best elk calls after having been bugled and chirped at hundreds of times over the span of several years.

Another big reason for less vocal elk, though, particularly in places like Idaho and Montana, has to do with the many predators in the area. The explosive growth in the wolf population has left elk extremely skittish.

The elk call to each other so they know each other's location, but it also gives away their location to any hungry wolf packs looking for a meal. Elk have now learned to be less vocal as a survival strategy against the wolf packs running rampant.

There are other predators to be wary of, too. Grizzlies and mountain lions hunt the same lands and are equally attracted to cow and calf calls, thinking they might find an easy meal.

I know of one hunter last year who barely escaped an encounter with a mountain lion that was stalking him as he was calling from behind some cover.

At the last minute, he poked his head around the brush thinking he might have heard an elk not too far away that responded to his call.

Instead, he about jumped out of his skin when he realized he was only mere feet away from a mountain lion that was about to pounce on what it thought was a cow elk mewing!

He had just enough time to draw on his bow and release an errant shot as the lion diverted at the last second once it realized its prey was a human, not an elk. Phew!

Predators aside, it's also important to keep in mind what season you're hunting in. Elk are far less vocal after the rut, so if you're doing some late season rifle hunting, don't be surprised if you don't hear too many elk bugling back.

That being said, there are still many situations in which elk calling is one of the best strategies to use to lure in that big bull you've been trailing.

Let's go over when and where it's definitely advantageous to use your elk calls.

Six Effective Elk Calling Strategies Bull Elk Can't Ignore

1. Two heads are better than one

Some of the most effective elk calling strategies require two people to execute.

If you're hunting with a partner, have a plan as to who will be the caller and who will be the shooter.

The best plans involve getting the caller to divert the attention of the bull elk so that his attention is focused on the caller and not the shooter.

With the caller stationed thirty or forty yards behind the shooter, you can often get the bull to walk right past the shooter for a clear broadside shot from a safe distance.

2. The lost cow/calf

When a herd bull is with his harem, it is extremely difficult to get him to leave it.

In these instances, you have to employ a more indirect tactic and call to the cows. If you make a call that sounds like a lost calf or cow, you can often get one of the other cows to come looking for it.

The herd bull will be keeping a close eye on his cow. Sometimes he'll follow her to gather her back. That's when you can make your shot.

3. Make him hot

A herd bull doesn't want any satellite bulls encroaching on his territory. If you've observed some ample distance between a herd bull and some of his cows, you can hit him with a whiny cow call. This is the sound a cow makes when it's being harassed by a bull.

This will get the herd bull's attention. Once he's interested, you can hit him with a young bull bugle to give realism to the scenario of a cow being harassed by a satellite bull, and this will often get the herd bull worked up enough to come your direction to run off the pesky satellite bull harassing his cows.

4. <u>Add natural sound effects</u>

Sometimes, an elk will sneak up on you. But more often than not, an elk is like a bull in a china shop that you'll hear coming from a long way off—they can be extremely noisy as they roam through the forest and brush.

In addition to trying to imitate their calls, you should also accompany those calls with appropriate ambient sound effects. Kick a rock down a slope, stomp around, step on twigs, rattle some antlers… anything to add realism to your setup.

5. <u>Late season calling</u>

While peak calling happens just before and during the rut, there are instances when late season calling can still be effective.

Remember that, later in the season, cows that didn't get bred during the peak rut will go back into estrous, creating a secondary rut.

Herd bulls will still be maintaining their harems, but young bulls will be in a state of desperation by this time. If you hit them with some estrus calls, you stand a chance of getting that young bull desperate to breed to move into your setup.

6. <u>Mind the wind</u>

Lastly, no matter how good your calling or setup is, it will be all for naught if that elk catches your scent.

Some hunters like to say that an elk will hear you three times, see you twice, but only smell you once.

When enacting your calling strategy, always know which direction the wind is coming from. A curious or agitated elk will always circle downwind of you when coming in to check out what's making the commotion. Be prepared for this, and position yourself accordingly both before and after the call.

If he catches wind of you, he'll hightail it out of there before you can even ready your shot.

There are dozens more strategies you can experiment with when trying to call in an elk or get him to give up his position.

In the end, elk calling comes down to experience. Experience with knowing how to use your call and experience in knowing when to use it. Every mistake is a new learning opportunity to put in your back pocket for later.

Over time, you'll have accumulated enough experiences and opportunities to be able to know when to use your call, which call to use, and which strategy is best based on the situation at hand.

Saving Private SNAFU

Despite the most detailed scouting missions and best laid battle plans, SNAFUs can and will occur.

SNAFU is a common military acronym that means "Situation Normal: All F-ed Up."

As any longtime elk hunter can tell you, just like in the military, things rarely go one hundred percent according to plan. Mother Nature, acts of God, and an uncooperative enemy can all torch plans that have been in the works for months and ruin a mission before it even gets started.

The same thing will happen when elk hunting as well. The best you can do is plan for the unexpected, be adaptable, and be ready for whatever comes your way.

In the meantime, you can make a mental checklist to be sure that you're not making any of the most common elk hunting mistakes that are sure to leave you eating tag soup year after year.

Five Surefire Ways to Ruin an Elk Hunt and Ensure You'll Be Eating Tag Soup for Dinner

1. <u>Only have a Plan A</u>

You studied the topographical maps and even managed to get out and scout the area once before the season started. Lots of fresh sign, plus you glassed a lot of elk not too far away. If this isn't elk heaven, you don't know what is!

But then opening weekend comes around and your idyllic elk refuge looks more like a haunted ghost town. You decide to camp out for a day and wait. You know they're there.

A day passes, and you still haven't seen nor heard an elk. Nothing is responding to your calls.

They'll be back, you tell yourself. Hunting requires patience, that's all.

Two days later, you walk out of the woods dejected with nothing to show for it but a sore back, bruised ego, and a bowl of tag soup to warm your belly.

This is what happens when you only have a Plan A. If elk hunting were easy, everyone would be doing it. But it's not. That's why you need not only a Plan A but plans B through Z as well.

Rarely does anyone get their elk with Plan A. Redundancy is where it's at—multiple plans of attack required should the first plans fail.

2. <u>Ignore the wind</u>

Pay no attention to thermals. Remain clueless as to which direction the prevailing winds come from. Feel the steady breeze at your back and the sunshine in your face. Enjoy your tag soup for dinner.

Hunters who don't heed the wind are hunters who go hungry quite often. Keep some form of wind check in your pack and use it to get a read on what the wind is doing. Know the prevailing wind and thermal patterns. Stay downwind of your target.

3. <u>Bugle often and continuously</u>

If they don't respond, they probably didn't hear you the first time. Keep blowing. Blow as you approach, too. Big bulls with a harem to protect love to hear you coming.

When all else fails, throw some Hoochie Mama at him. Nothing drives an elk wild like a loud Hoochie Mama call. The more frequent the better.

If you're not hoarse and deaf from calling all day, you're not doing it right!

The other hunters will thank you for driving all the elk their way.

You'll have some great stories to tell over a bowl of tag soup about all the ones that got away once your voice recovers from the all-day elk symphony you were conducting.

4. <u>Stick close to roads and trails</u>

The closer you are to a road or a trail, the easier it will be to haul that monster bull out after you shoot him! Stick within one to two miles of a road, and you'll be able to pack out your monster bull no trouble at all.

Glassing is easier from a vehicle. That way, you can stay warm in your truck as you keep a close eye out for big bulls frolicking in the meadows next to well-traveled roads.

Backcountry hunts are nice, but supper will be on the table at six p.m. and you told your wife you wouldn't be late…she's serving your favorite—tag soup!

5. <u>Only practice shooting in ideal conditions</u>

You're an ace at your local gun range sitting in your chair with your gun in its rest. You go out once a week, sit down, and fire your rifle at a paper target one hundred yards down a flat range.

You're totally ready to shoot at an elk on a steep forty-degree slope from a crouched position!

The only reason you missed is because the darn thing ducked a whole two feet at the last second, causing you to miss. He spooked, so you never got a second shot at him.

Oh well. Your shooting club is having a potluck next week. You'll bring your signature dish of tag soup to share with everyone while lamenting your poor luck (instead of your poor aim and lack of realistic preparation).

Hopefully you took note of the heavy dose of sarcasm within each of the above points.

In all seriousness, a survey of dozens of hunting guides revealed the above mistakes to be some of the most common that almost every hunter makes.

Be mindful that you're not making the same mistakes as listed above and work hard in the off-season to get better at what you know you're weakest at. Use each season as a new learning opportunity. Even with a lifetime of hunting under your belt, there is always something new to be learned!

Mission: Accomplished

It wasn't easy, but you did it!

There's no better feeling than that of Mission: Accomplished.

All the hard work. The drudgery. Weathering the elements. The mental uncertainty. Doubting yourself and your own resolve. Forging ahead anyway. Persevering. Winning!

Victory never tasted so sweet.

It's the stuff all great war stories are made of. You went into the wilderness prepared to battle it out and match wits with one of the most spectacular creatures in all of North America.

This time you were victorious. Other times you were humbled.

But one thing is for certain: hearing that elk bugle at you in the distance left you a changed man. That noise, similar to hearing your child cry for the first time, encapsulated your soul.

All the sleepless nights, the blistered feet, the sore back, the hunger pains…it's totally worth it in the end.

Next season is only eleven short months away, and you already can't wait!

Time to re-read this book and start preparing!

CLEAN IT

The Unconventional Yet Super Efficient Method to Elk Cleaning All the Hunting Pros Swear By

There's a saying in hunting, "The fun's over when you pull the trigger!" Truer words were never spoken, especially when doing any sort of big game hunting.

If elk meat weren't so darned delicious, I'm not so sure many people would even bother—I'd be totally cool with living off of venison, small game, and various bird species. But, gosh darn it, elk is mighty tasty. So tasty I served it at my wedding (you'll read more about that next chapter). It's all fun and games until you walk up to that 700 pound creature laying on the ground in 40 degree weather off the side of a steep mountain slope an hour before dusk 3 miles from where you parked your vehicle.

I wish I could tell you cleaning an elk will be easy—it's not, especially if it's your first one. That's why most people graduate to elk hunting only after they've done deer or other small game hunts for several seasons. Once you've done it a few times, it becomes significantly less arduous, especially if you have other experienced hunters in your group to show you the ropes.

In particular, there is one method that all the hunting pros swear by that will not only allow you to clean your elk more efficiently, but will enable you to bag more bulls as a result.

Traditions and Field Dressing an Elk

Time-honored traditions and best practices get passed down from hunter to hunter, generation to generation in the hunting world. Without these traditions, an important part of our heritage as humans would be lost, and we'd be trying to reinvent the wheel year after year.

At the same time, with improvements in technology and as society advances, there is a case to be made for breaking tradition when the time calls for it.

One of the long agreed upon traditions in hunting big game animals is the gutting of the animal. Everyone knows you must gut your animal as soon as possible to get the animal cooling down. I talked about how to do this in the deer section. The process is not any different for an elk: you cut around the sex organs (saving anything needed for proper ID as per state regulations), cut the anus, slice up the middle, remove the trachea, spill the belly and Bob's your uncle.

If you're new to elk hunting, this is a perfectly fine and probably the best way of doing it. But what if there were another way?

I know hunters get stuck in tradition a fair bit. It's the mentality that we do things a certain way because that's how we were taught.

Fair enough. That mentality has served us well for centuries. But when we know better, we do better. So I'm here to show you a better way to field dress your elk...*without even having to gut it!*

The #1 Secret to Shooting More Bulls on Public Lands

Successful guides and hunters get asked all the time how they shoot so many bulls on public lands.

Everyone knows public lands are difficult to hunt because they get significantly more pressure than private lands. Yet there are always a few people you know who seem to walk out with their bull tag filled year after year.

While there are certainly several reasons why those people are so successful, one of the more unsexy reasons is because they've adopted that bold mentality of venturing into unknown territory.

They're not afraid to hike in three or more miles whereas most hunters tend to stay within a few miles of a motorized trail. Naturally, there are far fewer elk within one to two miles of a motorized trail—they aren't stupid!

What emboldens the best hunters to fearlessly trek into the harshest of back country and come out with their tag filled every time?

I'll let you in on the secret…these types of hunters are well-versed in the "Mountain Top Butcher Shop" method of cleaning their elk. Once you relieve yourself of the fear of knowing what to do with your elk once you shoot it, a world of possibilities opens up before you.

_Learning the "Mountain Top Butcher Shop" method will allow you to pursue those bull elk well into the gnarliest territories of the deepest canyons. Master this technique and you will soon become the one walking out with your elk tag filled year after year while everyone else is scratching their head wondering how you did it.

So without further ado, it's time to learn how to field dress your elk in a way that's less messy, less smelly, more efficient, and doesn't require you to drag the animal or be close to your vehicle to winch it out.

The Mountain Top Butcher Shop Method for Field Dressing Your Elk

In case you haven't guessed from the name, the "Mountain Top Butcher Shop" method requires you to butcher the elk as it lies and pack the meat out. Many other hunters refer to it as the "gutless" method.

While you can gut your animal the traditional way, the good news is that, with this method, you can do all the butchering without having to gut the animal first. When you're in the field, having to deal with and work around those stinky, messy entrails and stomach can be utterly nauseating, not to mention the stench attracts flies. Plus, this method actually cools the meat down faster than if you were to field dress the elk the traditional way by gutting it.

There are a few essential items (in addition to your normal pack items) you will need in order to carry out the butcher shop method. These are:

- 2 good quality knives—a scalpel blade for more precise cuts and skinning plus a traditional blade for breaking joints and cutting thicker parts of the hide and neck

- Good quality game bags

- Latex gloves

- Headlamp

- Nylon cord

The Method

Now we're going to go over the basic steps of performing this method. As with anything in elk hunting, it's infinitely easier if you have a buddy or two with you to help hold the animal, hold the game bags, and generally assist as you take off the various parts of the elk—I wouldn't recommend doing this method solo if you've never done it before.

1. Secure the animal

If you're hunting steep territory, you'll want to use the nylon cord to secure the animal by its antlers or legs to a nearby tree or other sturdy object if possible to prevent it from sliding further downhill.

2. Skin the topside

With the elk on its side, start at the knee joint of the back leg and make an incision up the front of the leg to the belly. Continue up the belly to the armpit of the front shoulder. Finish your incision down the back of the front leg at the knee joint.

Once the primary incision is made, start skinning at the rear quarter. Continue skinning up the side of the elk all the way to the knee joint of the front shoulder, and remove the hide off of the front shoulder. Lift the skin off the entire side of the elk to the backbone, exposing as much meat as possible to the air to promote cooling.

Finish that side by continuing up the brisket and the neck to expose the front shoulder and neck meat.

3. Remove the hind quarter

If you have a buddy, have him hold the hind leg up as you begin cutting along the inside of the quarter. He should also have a game bag at the ready. If not, you can tie the leg to a tent stake or tree to keep it up in the air as you cut the inner thigh.

Decide whether you want to leave proof of sex intact on this side or the other one and work accordingly.

Locate the back edge of the pelvic bone and cut around it. Carry on down the edge of the pelvic bone like you're filleting a fish. Locate the ball socket where the leg meets the pelvic bone and pop that socket, then continue cutting the meat off the pelvic bone.

Next, locate the hipbone and follow it by cutting down toward the pelvic joint.

Now you can start working on the outer side of the quarter and cutting the meat away from the hip bone on the top side. Finish cutting the meat away from the quarter until it comes free and immediately place in a game bag. Try not to let the quarter touch the ground.

Place the bag with the meat in a shady and breezy area where it can keep cooling down.

4. Remove the front quarter

Make a guide cut around the shoulder blade on the outer side of the shoulder. Then lift up the leg and start cutting the underside of the shoulder along the ribs to detach the quarter.

Continue cutting the underside until you circle back to the original guide cut you made and then remove the shoulder from the body. Immediately place it in a game bag and set it aside with the other quarter.

5. Baby got backstrap

Locate the backstrap. Cut along the bottom side of the backstrap first, cutting it away from the topside of the ribs. Then start in on the topside of the backstrap and work your way down the backbone. Filet the meat off the backbone all the way to where it attaches to the neck. It might help to cut a small hole in the meat to grab onto while filleting. Place the meat immediately in a game bag.

6. Neck beard

Yes, the neck has plenty of edible meat on it as well. You don't want that to go to waste! This usually gets turned into burger so you don't have to be as precise with your cuts. Just do what you need to do working as methodically as possible to get the neck meat off the bone.

7. Don't forget the ribs!

Work down the side of the body removing as much meat as you can from the ribs and anything else you may have missed along the way.

You especially don't want to forget to remove the brisket from underneath the chest. That's some good meat right there!

8. Love me tenderloin

This is the most difficult cut to get to if you're a novice and presents the greatest risk to puncturing the stomach if you don't know what you're doing. The tenderloin lies on the underside of the backbone just in front of the hipbone.

Make a shallow incision along the backbone to expose the tenderloin. Be very careful not to puncture the stomach. Locate the front end of the tenderloin and cut it loose. From here, you can just use your hands to gently massage the tenderloin loose from the backbone. Cut the loin from the other end of the backbone.

9. <u>Roll over and repeat</u>

Roll the cape back over the exposed carcass, roll the animal over, and repeat the exact same steps on the other side. You can then easily get to the heart, liver, and tongue of the animal if you so choose.

It's okay to leave bloodshot meat behind. You don't want to be carrying the extra weight of blood clots that are just going to spoil the meat anyhow. If you need to cut out and around part of the front quarter, for instance, where the shot went through, don't worry about it.

10. <u>Off with its head!</u>

Lastly, you'll want to remove the head. This can be a bit tricky at first if you don't know what you're looking for. The good news is that you don't need a saw to take the head. You can remove it with your standard hunting knife.

Lift the head up from behind and point the nose down toward the ground. You're looking for the joint where the skull meets the top vertebra. Cut the excess meat around the base of the skull to more easily locate it.

Work your knife around that skull-spine joint area to cut all the soft tissue and membranes that hold the joint together. Once that's done, you can stand behind the head and use the antlers as leverage as you push or twist the head to break that joint.

Lastly, just cut away the rest of the tissue, muscle, and skin on the throat that's holding the head together.

All told, this part will probably take you a good couple of hours to get it all butchered, bagged up, and ready to pack out. You'll need a good head lamp with you in case you shot the bull late in the day.

Keep in mind, depending on where you shot the elk, it could also take you a couple of days to pack all the meat out as well.

Think of elk cleaning like a day of drinking. As I like to say, "It's a marathon, not a sprint!" If you know in advance and mentally prepare yourself that you're going to be at it for a while, then you can pace yourself accordingly. No need to try and do in an hour what you should allot several hours for!

Other Secrets of the Pros

Here are a few other tips to keep in mind for what to do with your elk during and after field dressing it:

- If you bag the game and keep it in a shady spot where a breeze can pass over it, you shouldn't have a problem with leaving it for a day or two while you pack everything out.

- If you're worried about other predators getting into your meat, use your nylon cord to hang your game bags from a tree limb fifty feet off the ground and a good distance away from the carcass of the animal.

- When skinning your animal, always cut with the grain of the hide, not against it.

- Keep like cuts of meat together in separate game bags: one bag for the front quarters, one bag for the rear quarters, one bag for rib meat and off cuts, one bag for tenderloin and backstrap, etc. This will help when it comes time to process it so you know which cuts are which.

- If you really need to save weight, consider de-boning the shanks as well. This will save a considerable amount of space and weight. If that's not such a huge consideration, then the elk shanks will make for excellent and nutritious bone broth or savory elk shank osso bucco!

Take Your Hunting Game to the Next Level by Improving Upon Tradition

Now you can fearlessly hunt the backcountry where all the big bulls are lurking just like the pros do. For some, this may be the first time you've ever heard of the Mountain Top Butcher Shop method to elk cleaning. For others, you may have heard of it but for have never gotten around to trying it.

It might be like finally getting that smart phone you always ridiculed until you actually get one and realize all the cool things it can do for you, and then you wonder how you ever lived without it in the first place.

Some people just like to do things the traditional way. That's fine. More power to them. But if you're ready to charge into the future and take your hunting game to the next level, learning this method is a must.

The good news is that this method works just as well on deer as it does on elk. If you're not quite ready for elk hunting yet, you can perfect the method on smaller game like deer.

When it comes to tradition, it matters. In this case, I think it's better to think of it not as breaking with the traditional method of gutting your game but rather improving upon it. Rest assured that you'll be on firm footing alongside many of the other best hunters in the field by perfecting this improved, more efficient method of game cleaning.

COOK IT

Mouthwatering Elk Recipes Suitable for Sunday Supper

Elk holds a special place in my heart and is probably my favorite game meat. It's like the filet mignon of the game meat world whereas venison is the ground beef (in my humble opinion).

I first encountered it up in Canada. My former husband and I were visiting just north of the Banff area near the Yoho National Park. We were staying at the lovely Cathedral Mountain Lodge. They had a small restaurant on premises due to the lack of other dining options in the area, and it was fabulous!

They served local and regional products as much as possible, featuring Canadian produce and wines. The restaurant also offered local game meat. It was there that I had my first elk meat experience, and it literally changed my life.

We were served delectable elk tenderloin medallions with a port wine and cherry jus. Heavenly! We loved it so much that, when it came time to plan our wedding, we decided that elk would be one of the main course offerings along with grouper. No beef or chicken for us—game meat or fish! Everyone loved it, too, surprisingly.

If done properly, elk is one of the game meats that can be more refined, at least with the premium cuts.

I'll share the recipe for the elk dish that we served at our wedding, plus the meal we were prepared at another hunting lodge in Colorado. We were able to take the tenderloin from the cow we had just shot mere hours before and have the chef on site prepare it for us that night. A truly incredible—and quite literal—field to table experience.

Wedding Elk: Grilled Elk Tenderloin With Blackberry Reduction

- 1 full elk tenderloin
- Salt and pepper
- Rosemary sprig
- 2 tbsp. of canola oil (high smoke point oil)

Blackberry Reduction Sauce

- 1 tbsp. butter
- 1 shallot, finely chopped
- 1/2 tsp. dried thyme
- 1/2 cup fruity red wine (pinot noir or merlot)
- 2/3 cup beef stock
- 1/4 cup fresh blackberries
- 2 tbsp. blackberry preserves
- 1 tbsp. butter, cold

Instructions:

1. Heat a skillet over high heat for 2 minutes.

2. Sprinkle elk tenderloin with salt and pepper.

3. Add oil to the skillet. Once shiny and slightly smoking, lower heat slightly to medium high and drop the tenderloin and rosemary sprig in the skillet.

4. Sear on all sides for a total of 8 minutes (don't overcook!) until a nice brown crust forms on the outside.

5. Remove from skillet and transfer to a plate to rest. Loosely tent with foil while resting.

6. While the tenderloin rests, reduce skillet heat to medium and add 1 tablespoon of butter to the same skillet along with the shallots and thyme. Cook until soft, around 2 minutes.

7. Add the wine back to the pan, scraping any brown bits from the bottom. Simmer and reduce wine by half.

8. Stir in the beef broth, blackberries, and blackberry preserves. Mash berries as you stir. Continue simmering until the sauce is thick enough to coat the back of a spoon.

9. Optional: you can pour the reduction through a fine mesh strainer if you want a smoother sauce with fewer blackberry seeds before adding last tbsp. of butter.

10. Remove from heat and swirl in the last tablespoon of butter.

This was the dish we served at our wedding. The head chef served it with a cipollini onion fingerling cake and roasted baby carrots. Delicious!

Of course, you don't have to be quite so fancy. Just some roasted potatoes, mashed potatoes or even mashed sweet potatoes will be fine. If you have any medium sized garden carrots with the stems cut to 1/2 inch, they will make for a lovely presentation on the plate for some nice color.

Elk pairs very well with fruity or slightly sweet sauces like the blackberry reduction above or the port wine and cherry jus from Cathedral Mountain Lodge that I mentioned before.

And, really, it should have some sort of sauce with it for a bit more additional flavor.

Smooth as Tennessee Whisky

Here's another delicious way to prepare your elk tenderloin with a totally different kind of sauce. It still has the zip that the elk needs to brighten up the meat even though it's not made with fruit.

Elk Tenderloin With Whisky Cream Sauce

- 1 elk tenderloin
- Steak seasoning
- Olive oil

Whisky Cream Sauce:

- 1 white onion, chopped
- 8 tbsp. of butter
- 1/2 cup of whisky
- 1 cup of beef broth
- 1/2 cup heavy cream
- 1/4 tsp. garlic powder
- Salt and pepper
- Optional: flour or corn starch

Instructions:

1. Drizzle elk tenderloin with olive oil. Rub tenderloin generously with your favorite steak seasoning.

2. While the seasoned tenderloin rests and comes to room temperature, caramelize your onions. Add the butter to a sauté pan over medium heat and add onions. Cooking them over a medium or medium-low heat allows them to caramelize nicely and concentrates their sugars.

3. Once the onions are translucent and lightly golden in color, add in the whisky. Simmer the whisky and onions together until mixture is reduced by half and the strong whisky smell subsides.

4. Stir in heavy cream and continue to simmer over medium-low heat. Reduce heat further if cream starts to boil rapidly.

5. Add in salt, pepper, and garlic powder to taste and allow mixture to continue to reduce down. Mixture should be thick enough to coat the backside of a spoon.

6. If mixture does not seem to be getting thick, whisk in a tablespoon of flour or corn starch to thicken it up.

7. Heat your grill or your skillet to medium high heat. Allow it to heat for a couple of minutes before adding meat.

8. Add meat to heated grill or skillet and cook for 4-6 minutes per side. Spoon extra oil and seasonings on elk as needed while cooking.

9. Remove elk from heat, cover with foil, and allow to rest for 5-10 minutes. Meat continues to cook internally even after it's removed from heat.

10. Cut against the grain and serve with whisky cream sauce drizzled on top.

Again, I'd like to emphasize the importance of not overcooking your game meat. If you take the meat off the grill or out of the pan and it still looks pretty rare, throw it back on for another 2 minutes to bring it up to that medium rare temperature. But there's nothing you can do about it if it's already overcooked. I do not recommend cooking elk tenderloin above a medium rare if at all possible.

The elk with whisky cream sauce would go well served over some mashed potatoes or even some short noodles like penne, orzo, or egg noodles.

Two-hour Elk: From Field to Table in Two Hours or Less

The next recipe I'm going to share comes at you from my experience hunting elk in Colorado. I wasn't the one hunting, but I was along on the hunt with my former husband on some private property owned by an exclusive hunting lodge called Elk Creek Ranch.

We were driving along with the property owner and spotted some cows 200 yards away in the distance. The light was fading so it was a now or never opportunity.

We creeped up toward a slightly elevated hill as the cows were grazing in a field near a tree line.

My husband readied his shotgun, picking out the cow he was aiming for. All of a sudden, our guide accidentally dropped his eyeglasses on a rock on the ground beneath him.

The elk immediately looked up, spooked. Several of them started heading for the tree line already. It looked like we might have missed our shot. One of them got just inside the tree line, but not far enough. It turned broadside just long enough to take a look in our general direction.

My husband exhaled half a breath and fired. BOOM! A direct hit. I watched it fall on the spot and roll down the hill. My husband, whose eye was still to the scope of his rifle, didn't see what happened to the elk. Our guide still hadn't managed to put his eyeglasses back on so he couldn't see what happened to the elk.

I was the only one able to provide visual confirmation that the elk dropped dead on the spot and rolled down the hill. Of course, that meant that I was going to have to be the one to go and locate the elk while the other two went back for the truck and ATV.

I thought nothing of it at the time. I was happy to volunteer and be a contributing member of the hunt. Of course, it never occurred to me that I might be in danger myself from some other hungry predators out at dusk in search of their meal. But, as they say, ignorance is bliss!

When I found the elk, it was laying with its chest propped up on a rock jutting up out of the hillside facing downslope, as if it were placed there just ready and waiting for photo opportunities.

We gutted it, hooked it up to the ATV, and winched the animal onto the truck. We took it back to the ranch where we hung it up and immediately started skinning and cleaning it. Naturally, we had to take the tenderloins off right away to take back to the lodge where the chef prepared it straight away.

Now that's about as field to table as it gets! We enjoyed a delicious meal of elk tenderloin off an elk that had only been shot no more than two hours before.

The chef prepared the elk simply, but exquisitely, on a salad of simple greens but finished with a zesty and sweet balsamic glaze.

Here's a quick and easy salad you can whip up for elk tenderloin (elk flank steak works, too, but should be marinated ahead of time to tenderize).

Sweet as Balsamic Wine Vinegar

Elk and Mixed Greens Salad With Balsamic Dressing

- Mixed salad greens
- Thinly sliced red onion
- Dried cranberries
- Avocado, cut in chunks or sliced
- Blue cheese crumbles
- Toasted walnuts, pecans, or sliced almond (extra credit: can died spiced pecans)
- Sliced radish (optional)
- Elk tenderloin
- Salt and pepper
- Olive oil
- Balsamic glaze (optional)

Balsamic Dressing:

- 3/4 cup olive oil
- 1/4 cup balsamic vinegar
- 1 tbsp. honey
- Salt and pepper
- 1/4 tsp. dried Italian herbs

Instructions:

1. Put salad ingredients in a large bowl.

2. Season elk tenderloins with salt and pepper. Heat 2 tbsp. of olive oil over medium high heat on stove. Once oil is hot,

add tenderloin to the skillet and brown evenly on all sides, approximately 8-10 minutes for a nice medium rare (you can always return to skillet if it needs more cooking).

3. Let tenderloin rest for a couple minutes, then slice against the grain.

4. Make dressing. Whisk together all ingredients except the oil. Once all ingredients have been mixed, slowly drizzle in the olive oil a little bit at a time while continually whisking. Alternatively, you can throw all ingredients into a mason jar, seal tightly, and shake vigorously. Taste and adjust seasonings as necessary.

5. Drizzle a few tablespoons of dressing on salad and toss. Place salad on plates. Top with tenderloin medallions. Drizzle whole salad and elk with zig-zags or circles of balsamic glaze, if using. Otherwise, top elk with a spoonful of balsamic dressing and then serve!

As mentioned above, you can do this same salad with other cuts of elk like flank steak or sirloin. I would recommend that you marinate these cuts in a balsamic marinade or other marinade before cooking to tenderize the meat.

This makes a great lunch salad or light dinner. I highly recommend the balsamic glaze as an extra punch of flavor. It elevates the presentation of the salad as well.

If you don't have the glaze in a store near you, it's really easy to make. All you have to do is put a couple cups of balsamic vinegar in a saucepan over low heat and let it reduce until it's thick enough to coat the back of a wooden spoon. It keeps well in a cupboard and enhances a wide variety of foods, from pork to salmon to roasted veggies and even fruit skewers. Give it a try!

Fiesta!

Lastly, I just want to share an easy way to use your elk steaks.

A lot of people think that if it's a steak, they have to eat it that way, meaning rubbed in steak seasoning and thrown on the grill, eaten as is.

That's okay, but if I'm honest, sometimes it leaves a little something to be desired. Elk "steaks" aren't quite as thick and flavorful as a beef steak. Even the lowly sirloin steak from a cow at least has some substance to it, even if it's a bit chewy.

I think a better way to use up those elk steaks is to have a little Mexican fiesta in your mouth. Slice those bad boys up and make some fajitas out of them! They're the perfect size to slice into fajita sized strips of meat and sizzle away in a skillet.

Add in some spices, guacamole, and sour cream, and you've got yourself a party!

Elk Fajitas

- 6-8 elk steaks, sliced in strips
- 1 red pepper, sliced
- 1 yellow pepper, sliced
- 1 white onion, sliced lengthwise
- 6 tbsp. chili powder, divided
- 3 tbsp. ground cumin, divided
- 2 tbsp. ground paprika, divided
- 1 tsp. garlic powder
- 1/4 tsp. cayenne pepper
- Salt and pepper
- 6 tbsp. canola oil, divided

Instructions:

1. In a medium sized bowl, combine the sliced elk steaks, 4 tablespoons of chili powder, 2 tablespoons cumin, 1 tablespoon of paprika, garlic powder, cayenne, salt and pepper to taste, and 4 tablespoons of canola oil. Toss to coat.

2. In a separate medium bowl, combine peppers, onions, 2 tablespoons chili powder, 1 tablespoon cumin, 1 tablespoon paprika, salt and pepper to taste, and 2 tablespoons canola oil. Toss to coat.

3. Heat a large skillet over high heat for 2 minutes. Once skillet is hot, toss in elk meat coated in oil and spices. Sauté for 6-8 minutes or until elk is cooked through and browned on the outside. Once meat is cooked, remove from pan and place in serving dish. Cover to keep warm.

4. In same skillet, toss in the pepper and onion mixture. Sauté 6-8 minutes or until onions are translucent and peppers are cooked through.

5. Serve with your favorite Mexican accompaniments: hard/soft taco shells, shredded cheese, sour cream, guacamole, diced tomato, salsa, hot sauce, etc.

You can play with the spice mixture and proportions. This is just a general guideline. I prefer to use my own spice mixture as opposed to the taco packets you can buy in the store because I don't like all the preservatives they put in those packets. If taco packets make your life easier, use them!

This is just a fun, different way to use up elk steaks. Of course, eating them as a traditional steak should always be part of the dinner rotation. But throwing in a little fajita action now and then is a great way to add variety. It gets you out of the rut of just cooking elk like a run-of-the-mill steak. Think outside the box!

Your Sunday Supper

This should give you a good jumping off point for what to do with your massive elk haul the next time you bag a bull or cow.

Out of the most commonly hunted game meats, elk is almost certainly the most delicious. If you're going to take your time and make a special dinner out of one type of game meat, let elk be it.

Growing up with a single mom, we got a lot of boxed meals. But one thing we got special was Sunday dinner. I always looked forward to Sunday dinners because I knew we would usually get a nice, home-cooked meal that day. A nice pot roast or mom's famous chicken divan or a homemade macaroni and cheese, not just boxed.

Let elk be your "Sunday" meal (even if it's not actually cooked on Sunday). The one that is lovingly prepared, one that the family looks forward to, and one that truly honors the bounty and sacrifice the animal gave to you.

PART TWO
UPLAND BIRDS

Chapter Three

QUAIL & PHEASANT

HUNT IT

Bob White and the Curious Case of the Covey Rise

There once was a hunter named Bob. Bob was fairly new to hunting, but he had a bunch of friends who were into it and he thought he would give it a try.

Since he didn't grow up hunting, he wasn't sure if he would like it, although he did love shooting guns at the range every once in a while. He had an old pump action shotgun that he bought cheap off a buddy. Bob didn't want to buy a new gun, so he researched what kind of hunting he could do with the gun he had.

After doing a bit of browsing on the internet, Bob decided he'd like to give quail hunting a try. It seemed like something that would be fairly easy for a beginner to get involved with since it didn't need a ton of gear to get started. He didn't want to be stuck with items he didn't need if he decided he didn't like it.

Bob asked some friends of his if he could tag along on their next hunting trip, since he knew they were avid bird hunters. They agreed on a date the following week.

Bob realized he might need to pick up a few gear essentials. He stopped in at his local sporting goods store and picked out all the latest and most fashionable lightweight, breathable, moisture wicking UV-protected outdoor gear he could find.

Hat, sunglasses, shirt, slacks, shoes, and socks—he had all the latest and greatest products. He was ready to hunt!

The morning of the hunt, Bob turns up at the meeting point. He's feeling mighty impressed with himself as he steps out of his vehicle decked out in the best gear. They exchange greetings, ready themselves, let the dogs loose, and away they go!

After trudging in the fields all morning with barely any action, they finally decided to try the field over yonder to see if they can get more action. Almost as soon as they walk over there, they hear the tell-tale sound of the Bobwhite quail in the distance. Game on!

They quietly follow their dogs as they sniff around them in a tight zigzag pattern. One of them freezes at the base of a bushy shrub, its tail outstretched straight as an arrow. The four hunters line up as they wait to send in their flush dog. They let the spaniel loose and up pops six quail.

They unleash a spray of ammo and knock down four of the six birds. Bob isn't sure but he doesn't think he hit any. What a rush! He's ready to find some more.

They retrieve their downed birds and continue stalking the land. Not too much further away, their pointer goes stick straight again and starts to quiver. He's on to some!

As they did the last time, the hunters get in position. This time, the dog is pointing at a large patch of some tall cover grass. Once they're ready, they let the flush dog loose again. All of a sudden, a huge mass of birds rises from ground. Birds are flying everywhere in a chaotic frenzy.

Bob swings his gun from side to side in almost a total 180 degree arc, unsure of where to aim at. He fires twice into the cloud of birds, his heart pumping wildly, thinking that at this close range with this many birds he's bound to hit at least one.

Just as the flurry dies down, two last stragglers rise from the ground and try and make a beeline just above the cover. Bob, feeling startled and surprised, reflexively swings his gun in the direction of the escaping quail and takes one last shot at them hoping to prevent their escape, narrowly missing the flush dog that had spooked them out of their hiding spot.

"What the heck, Bob!" one of his buddies yelled, anger apparent in his voice.

"What do you think you're doing? You almost shot Birdie Boop!" his other friend shouted incredulously.

The hunters shook their heads in disapproval and lectured Bob about gun safety for a few minutes before they resumed their hunt. Bob was sure that, after all that, he still didn't manage to shoot down any birds.

They continued hunting for a couple more hours. While Bob was much more disciplined with his shotgun after the stern lecture he received earlier, he was hardly more accurate. By the day's end, Bob had only shot one bird, and the shot barely clipped it. It was his buddy's shot that actually took it out.

After starting the day excited for the hunt and feeling like a million bucks in his new hunting gear, Bob finished the day feeling dejected and questioning if he even wanted to give this hunting thing another go.

What did Bob do wrong? What could he have done better to improve his shooting and down more birds? How could Bob have gotten more enjoyment out of his hunt and been a better hunting partner to his buddies?

We'll discover the answers to these questions as we delve into the mystery of Bob White and the Curious Case of the Covey Rise. Not only that, we'll learn how the answers to this mystery apply not just to quail hunting but pheasant hunting as well.

Put on your detective hat and let's get to the bottom of this mystery!

Birds of a Feather...

Quail and pheasant hunting is similar enough that they can be lumped together in one chapter. They're both found in open, grassy bushland and fields where they have enough cover from predators trying to get them.

Quail is largely found in the southeastern United States, specifically the bobwhite quail, to which I am primarily referring to in this chapter.

There are other, lesser known, species of quail. These species include:

• **Scaled quail**

Found in Texas, New Mexico, Colorado, and Kansas

• **California quail**

Found in California and other parts of the west coast

• **Gambel's quail**

Found in southwest desert

• **Mountain quail**

Found in Oregon coastal mountains down through Southern California

• **Montezuma's quail**

Found in New Mexico desert highlands

Pheasant is more of a northern and midwestern bird. The most common pheasant in the U.S. is the ring-necked pheasant. It's distinguished by a white ring around the neck separating its blue and red head from its brown-feathered body.

Wild pheasant is primarily found in the Dakotas, Kansas, Iowa, Missouri, Nebraska, and a few other surrounding states.

Of course, many states have hunting clubs with farmed pheasant that they use to stock the land. If you're looking to shoot some game bird, you don't have to head to the middle states to bag some bird—there's usually a stocked hunting club just a few hours away.

Did you know that the state bird of South Dakota is the Ring-necked pheasant?

The Right Tools for the Job

Bob's instincts were correct in knowing that he would need some essential gear before heading out for his hunt.

Unfortunately, he was wooed by the nice looking mannequins in the store and went with form over function when it came to being properly outfitted for his hunt.

There are a few essential tools for those wanting to get into upland bird hunting. The good news is there are far fewer things needed for quail and pheasant hunting than for other game hunts.

To get you started with upland bird hunting, here's the bare minimum to get you started:

- 12 Gauge or 20 Gauge shotgun

- #6 or #7-1/2 shotgun shells

- Blaze orange safety gear

- Bird bag / ammo bag

- Hunting dog (not required but strongly recommended)

- Comfortable shoes and pants

Size Doesn't Matter—It's All in How You Use It

There continues to be some spirited disagreement about what gauge shotgun is best for upland bird hunting. While both a 12 gauge and a 20 gauge (16 gauge as well) work just fine, there are definite opinions on both sides of the equation.

Bottom line is that a 20-gauge shotgun is generally smaller and lighter than its 12 gauge counterpart. The 20 gauge also typically has less recoil, which makes it a great option for new hunters.

Due to its size and weight, 20-gauge shotguns are often recommended for female and youth hunters. It's easier to carry for long periods of time and the reduced recoil makes it optimal for those more sensitive to recoil.

The downside of this, however, is that with a smaller gun comes a smaller shot. There is less birdshot fired at the bird and it doesn't travel quite as far. In short, you have to be more accurate with a 20 gauge to increase your chances of hitting your target.

With a 12 gauge, you get more power and more pellets per shot, so your likelihood of shooting a bird is greater. For this reason, it has grown in popularity over the 20 gauge throughout the years, particularly as manufacturers have found ways to reduce the weight and recoil of some 12 gauges.

Could Bob's shotgun have caused him to miss so badly when it came time to down some quail?

In retrospect, Bob recalls that his friend who gave him the gun said it used to be his wife's but that she didn't use it anymore. Even though he enjoyed shooting guns, Bob wasn't very well-versed on the technical aspects of guns yet. He failed to take notice of the fact that the gun he got cheap off his buddy was a 20 gauge, not a 12 gauge. Having barely shot it, Bob was not nearly as accurate with it as he needed to be given the smaller loads the 20 gauge was firing.

This was one of Bob's first "aha!" moments when trying to figure out why he shot so few birds on his first ever quail hunt.

Ammo, Ammo

Once you know what kind of gun you'll be shooting with, next up is deciding which kind of ammo you need for your gun. While there are a few considerations to keep in mind while choosing your ammo, the most important one is pellet size number. This will be the last number on the right on a box of shotgun shells.

Pellet size number refers to the number of pellets per shotgun shell. The more pellets there are per shell, the smaller the pellet itself is. Shells range from #9—the smallest—all the way down to BB size—the largest. Naturally, you want the size of your shell to match the size of the game you're shooting. Quail, being a smaller game bird, is going to require a bigger number of lead shot (#7-1/2 to #9).

You can get away with a #8 or #9 on quail, especially in private hunts on stocked land where you'll be at close range to a lot of birds. But more commonly used on quail is a #7-1/2. The #7-1/2 is a good all-around shot because it works on everything from dove to pheasant.

For pheasant, more common would be a #6, sometimes even a #5 being that they're slightly larger birds than quail are. If you can get close to a pheasant, a #7-1/2 is fine. The problem with pheasant is they like to run.

Unlike a quail that will hunker down and hope you don't see them—or the dogs don't find them—a pheasant's instinct is to run away. That's why they like lands with high brush cover because, even if you have a dog pointing on a spot, they might have snuck off and are already tens of yards away before you, or the dog, notice it's even taken off. At that point, you're going to have to hope your dog catches up or you're going to have to take a longer shot, which will require heavier duty ammo to impart a fatal blow. You're going to have to walk the line of making sure you have powerful enough ammo to make the shot from whatever distance you're shooting at but not too powerful that you blow the bird to smithereens. In that case, you've ruined a perfectly good bird, and that's one less you get to take home and eat for dinner!

The next part to solving the mystery of Bob White is knowing whether he was using the right ammo.

When his friend sold him that gun, he also gave Bob a couple boxes of ammo for it as well. Bob, always a sucker for a deal, was stoked that he wouldn't have to go out and buy any ammo for the gun. He thought he was getting a package deal and feeling pretty lucky at how cheaply he was getting all of it for!

Bob looked on the box of ammo and realized the box of shells he received were #8s—still within reason for a quail hunt. Being later in the season when the birds have more feathers, perhaps this, plus using a less powerful 20 gauge, is why his shot wasn't a kill shot on the one bird he managed to clip.

Bird Dogs—A Hunter's Best Friend

There are certain birds at certain times of year that you'll be able to find without the aid of dog. But for the other ninety percent of the time, if you're serious about your bird hunting, you're going to want to get your own bird dog.

The good news is that, by and large, almost all breeds of bird dogs also make excellent family pets. Don't let their ferocity in the field fool you. Most of these dogs are sweet, loving, gentle dogs that love cuddles and are excellent with children.

Some of the most common breeds of bird dogs are:

- Labrador Retriever
- Golden Retriever
- German Shorthaired Pointer
- Brittany (formerly known as a Brittany Spaniel)
- Boykin Spaniel
- English Springer Spaniel
- English Setter
- English Pointer
- Irish Red and White Setter
- Red Setter
- Nova Scotia Duck Tolling Retriever

Each of these dogs is bred for a different type and style of hunting. It's important that you do some research into each breed to determine which is best for whatever kind of game you most like to hunt and that suits your home environment.

Did you know that a German Shorthaired Pointer named CJ was awarded Best in Show at the 2016 Westminster Dog Show?

The Right Dog for the Job

There's a lot that goes into training a bird dog. Each type of dog requires different training methods based on the breed characteristics. Training of bird dogs is beyond the scope of this book, but once you do have a well-trained, fully developed bird dog, you're in for years of fun and camaraderie—the bond between man and dog during such a high stakes and high adrenaline activity as hunting is indescribable and will provide for a lifetime of memories.

The fun really begins when your dog develops its hunting personality and you learn to adjust your hunting strategy based on how your bird dog hunts. That's when you'll really become a dynamic duo.

For instance, one dog, like our Brittany, might be a very fast and agile dog that can cover a lot of ground. It will find birds for long stretches of land, but due to the large amount of ground it covers is prone to missing birds along the way. Once you know this, you can adjust your strategy to hunt the same stretch of land up and back to allow your dog to find birds it might have missed the first time.

A Boykin Spaniel, for instance, might hunt in tight circles around you. If there's a bird within a thirty-foot radius of you, it's not going to miss it. Of course, you won't cover as much ground this way but its efficient hunting style means you won't have to.

Bob was unprepared for having to shoot over dogs. In his haste to make a shot, he forgot about the presence of the flush dog, took a shot level with the horizon, and barely missed the flush dog. A close call like that is not something Bob will likely forget any time soon.

Best Ways to Bag Some Field Chicken

Now that we've discussed some of the gear essentials, we're ready to dive into what you actually need to do to get you some field chicken for dinner.

First and foremost, it's important to have a strategy. Since it was his first time hunting for quail, Bob didn't have much to contribute to the strategy sessions, but he was very interested in hearing the plans laid forth by his buddies as they were discussing the best plan of attack for the day.

Bob was making mental notes during the strategy sessions. Some of the important things discussed were as follows:

1. Survey the lay of the land

Note which direction the wind is coming from. This was important so that they knew how to hunt the dogs. Dogs work best hunting into the wind where they can catch wind of scents more easily.

2. Know your dogs

Take into account the time of day and how long you are going to be hunting for. Be mindful of your dog's limitations. Let your dogs' strengths and weaknesses play into your strategy.

His buddies had been quail hunting for the better part of a decade. They knew it would be better to hunt their older, larger dogs early in the morning. When they were younger and stronger, they were much better equipped to handle the warmer parts of the day. Now that they were older, they excelled in the cooler morning weather.

3. Evaluate your strategy

When your dogs take a rest, that's a great time to re-evaluate your strategy. If it's not working, change it up.

One thing Bob's buddies found strange was that they weren't hearing any quail. Most people know the telltale sound a Bobwhite quail makes, but his buddies were experienced enough to know their other noises and whistles as well.

When they weren't seeing or hearing much of anything in the current field they were hunting, they decided to try another field.

Bob thought it was smart to stop every so often and listen for birds. His buddies kept telling him, if you're not seeing, hearing, or finding any birds—then, hey, maybe there's no birds.

There's Birds in Them Thar Fields!

Your strategy is in place. You've let your dog loose in the field and all of a sudden you see him go as motionless as a statue—bird on!

Unfortunately, nobody had prepped Bob for what can happen during a covey rise. His adrenaline got the better of him, he lost his wits, didn't control his shotgun, and became a huge safety hazard during the wild frenzy of the covey rise.

After the heat of the moment had passed, his buddies reminded him of these key rules whenever they were about to have a shot at some birds.

- Approach the dog slowly from behind.

- Make sure you are aware of where all dogs and hunters are. Make sure other hunters are safely behind the line of fire and there's plenty of blue sky between your muzzle and the ground as you get ready to shoot.

- If you have a partner, be sure you know where each other's line of fire is and that you're not crossing the mid-line and shooting into your partner's territory.

- Survey the situation and make an educated guess as to which way the birds are going to fly. Typically they will fly downwind.

- Once safety has been established, send in your flush dog, stomp your foot, or kick some branches a few times to get the birds to rise.

- Ready, aim, and fire!

What to Expect When You're Expecting to Shoot Some Birds

Bob didn't know what to expect on his first quail hunt. Despite doing some research on the internet, there's no comparison to the adrenaline rush you get in the field. He got flustered and just shot indiscriminately into the swirl of birds as they were flying away, hoping that one of his pellets would find a target.

While lamenting his poor success after the fact to his buddies, one of them revealed the simple reason Bob was so inaccurate.

"You didn't implement the 'Pick It and Stick It' technique, that's why," his buddy informed him.

"The 'Pick It and Stick It' technique? What's that?"

"Listen and learn, my friend."

Pick It and Stick It

The 'Pick It and Stick It' technique is simple: when the covey rises, pick one bird and aim for that one bird rather than take a general shot at the whole covey.

Bob learned that rather than shooting aimlessly into the cloud of birds, he still needed to be focused on one bird in particular and aiming directly at it, rather than aiming at the swarm in general and just hoping he catches one.

Pheasant

As Bob and his friends were rehashing the hunt, the conversation turned to pheasant hunting. Just like with quail hunting and how a covey rise can be startling for someone on their first go, there are a couple things to be aware of when hunting pheasant as well.

"Pheasant are sneaky, and it takes a little bit more effort to outsmart those suckers," his friend said with a gleam in his eye.

He continued, "Part of the reason they're sneaky is because unlike a quail that will sit and hunker down and hope you don't see them, a pheasant will run off on you without getting airborne—and those suckers are fast!"

Another buddy chuckled and said, "Either that or they'll fly off on you before you even get close enough to shoot one! Man, I hate when that happens!"

Bob's buddies warned him that one thing to beware of is that pheasant can startle you when they flush. Kind of like the frenzy of a covey rise with quail can startle you and cause you to get flustered, rush your shot, and miss, a pheasant makes a terrifying noise as it flushes which, if you're not prepared for it, can scare the bejesus out of you.

One guy put it like this: "Just think of it like your ex-wife or ex-girlfriend—you know she's gonna come at you screeching. Don't let psycho pheasant throw you off your game. Just take a step back, adjust your sights, take note of the bird's flight pattern, swing the gun at the white neck ring and shoot."

"If you miss, then your ex-wife wins!" one guy joked. "Just think of it like that and you'll never miss a shot again in your life!"

They all had a good laugh at that as they downed the last of their beers. Bob was grateful he was finally getting down to the nitty gritty of what it takes to be a good upland bird hunter.

The #1 Secret to Becoming a Better Bird Hunter

Bob was starting to feel better about his hunt that day. Despite some low moments, he was enjoying the camaraderie with his friends. Not to mention watching the dogs work was utterly fascinating.

Thinking he'd like to give upland bird hunting another go, he asked his friends for some honest advice.

"All right. So what is it I need to do if I want to be as good at hunting birds as you guys are?"

His friends kind of looked at each other, seeing who would be the one to deliver the painful truths.

Finally one of them turned to him and said, "It might seem like I'm stating the obvious here but the best way to become a better bird hunter is to become a better shooter...

You can have all the gadgets and gizmos and latest clothing items from fancy stores that you want, but none of that is going to do the most fundamental part of hunting for you—shooting the bird out of the sky."

Bob let that sink in for a moment before he asked, "Ok, well what does that entail?"

"What does that entail? Well, #1 it means knowing your shotgun."

His friend knew that Bob had only recently acquired his new shotgun. Knowing that, he was pretty certain that Bob had probably barely shot it before having gone on their hunt.

His friend carried on with the advice.

"Ideally, before you even go on your first quail or pheasant hunt, you'll have already shot your shotgun many times. This could be at a local trap and skeet club or, if you live in a rural enough area, even in your own backyard.

There are also lots of drills you can do at home with an unloaded shotgun that will help improve your shooting and accuracy. The easiest of these is to just practice swinging and mounting an unloaded shotgun to your shoulder several times a day a few days a week.

Professional and Olympic shooters do this drill up to two hundred times a day. Not only does it build muscle memory but it helps build the muscle itself so that it doesn't fatigue and cause you to miss as you get tired near the end of the day."

Wow! Again, Bob was floored by how easy, yet how practical the advice was.

One of the others threw in his two cents as well. "My favorite drill is the Flashlight Drill."

"The flashlight drill?" Bob asked as he raised an eyebrow.

"Yeah, sure. Take a small flashlight and fit it inside the barrel of your gun. A Maglite AA fits nicely inside of a 12-gauge shotgun and a AAA fits inside of a 20 gauge.

Twist the light on to its narrowest setting in a darkened room. Train your light on the top corner of the room and stand in a ready position. Mount the gun smoothly so the light never wavers from that spot. Then practice just swinging the gun back and forth as if shooting crossing shots, keeping the beam on the seam between the wall and the ceiling.

Finally, put it all together starting from a ready position. Practice mounting your gun while keeping your light trained on the same spot on the wall and then move the muzzle along the flight of imaginary bird."

"Bob, I guarantee you that if you just start practicing these two drills at least a couple times a week, by the next time we go out, you'll be knocking 'em down left and right!"

Bob could already feel the excitement rise in his chest. He knew now what he had to do and couldn't wait to get started.

The #1 Mistake You're Making When Hunting Upland Bird

Bob's friend had one last piece of advice to share before he was done with him though.

"Bob, I've been bird hunting for over a decade now. I've taken a lot of people out on hunts. By and large, the biggest mistake most hunters make when hunting quail and pheasant is not getting their shotgun mounted."

"What do you mean by that?" Bob asked, a little puzzled.

"Well, it's an exciting situation when you flush a covey of quail or a pretty rooster from the brush, plus it all happens very quickly. In the excitement of the moment, most hunters just swing their gun in the general direction of the bird or birds and pull the trigger hoping that some of the birdshot will find a home in breast of one of those birds.

Nine times out of ten, the hunter will be disappointed. In addition to everything else we've talked about, they failed to properly mount their guns before they even got the shot off."

"When you say 'failed to properly mount their gun,' what does that mean exactly?" Bob still wasn't completely comprehending.

"The best way to combat that disappointment and start bagging more birds is with what I like to call the 'Mount It to Count It' Technique."

Bob leaned in as he listened intently to his friend describe the 'Mount It to Count It' technique.

Mount It to Count It

Bob's friend described the technique:

"This is actually a very easy technique to master.

1. Mount the gun

2. See the bird

3. Shoot the bird

Notice which part comes first in that process: mount the gun. Mount the gun first. Then pick out a bird. One specific bird. Shoot that bird. Too many hunters reverse the order. They see the bird they want to shoot, throw the shotgun muzzle up, pull the trigger and it usually goes ten feet over the bird's head.

If you haven't mounted that shotgun on your shoulder and gotten your cheek resting on the stock, that muzzle is well above your line of sight.

Mounting the gun isn't just bringing the gun to your shoulder. It's resting your cheek on the stock as well. This ensures that your muzzle is aligned with your line of sight as you keep your eyes locked on your target.

"If you combine the 'Mount It to Count It' technique with the 'Pick It and Stick It' technique, you'll be a bird hunting pro in no time, Bob."

He could hardly wait!

The Mysterious Case of the Covey Rise: CLOSED

By most measures, Bob had a pretty disastrous first upland bird hunt.

- He risked the safety of both his hunting partners and the dogs by not following proper safety procedures.

- He was unfamiliar with his gun and ammunition and therefore was unaware of how it would perform or what to expect from it.

- He was unprepared for the excitement and rush that can come from a covey rise and allowed himself to take hurried, unfocused shots.

- As a result of all this, he walked away from a full day's hunt having only wounded one bird. His ego was more bruised than the bird was.

The good news is, he took his buddies' hunting advice to heart. The next day he started practicing some of the drills they told him about. He spent ten minutes just doing shoulder mounts and getting used to raising and lowering his shotgun. Boy did that give his shoulder a workout!

After that, he tried out the flashlight drill his buddy told him about. He was surprised at how hard it was to keep the flashlight trained on one spot as he mounted his shotgun. After some practice, he became much steadier and got fairly good at remaining balanced as he mounted the gun to his shoulder and swung the muzzle.

He managed to repeat these drills three more times over the next week and a half before his next hunt. When the day came for the next hunt, Bob stepped out of his vehicle looking like a million bucks as before but notably more nervous. He was worried that, despite his practice, he wouldn't perform any better than last time.

They got out in the field and were immediately more successful at finding birds than they were the last time. Cujo was on point. At his buddy's word, they sent in Birdie Boop to flush the birds.

Here goes nothing, thought Bob.

Up flew four birds. Bob had already taken note of the wind direction and was fairly certain he knew in which direction the birds were likely to fly. He got his shotgun mounted like he had been practicing. He recalled his buddy's "Pick It and Stick It" technique and honed in on the one bird that was safely within his target range.

He took aim and BOOM! Dropped it! Bob was elated. His practice had paid off immediately.

The day carried on and although Bob still missed his fair share of birds, he did manage to bring down a few birds by day's end. His buddies were thoroughly impressed with his improvement since their last hunt praised him at the end of the day.

"Great work, Bob!" one remarked.

"Yeah, man. Good shooting today," his other buddy commended him.

"Now we just have to teach you how to clean these suckers up!"

Bob was already ready for the challenge. You'll be, too, as you learn quick and easy techniques for cleaning your upland bird.

CLEAN IT

Winning Ways to Quickly Clean Quail and Pheasant

Now that you've successfully shot and killed some birds, it's time to clean those feathery messes up.

Everyone has a different technique for cleaning their birds. It depends on how you like to eat them. Some people just want the breast, where most of the meat is. Others like the whole bird so they can roast it in the oven. Some people like the skin on while others think it takes too much time to pluck the feathers so they take the skin off.

If you're new to quail and pheasant, it's a good idea to try a few different ways of cleaning your game until you determine your preferred way to eat and clean them. Once you get good at it, you can get the basic cleaning of a pheasant done in under three minutes and a quail in under two minutes.

The Basics of Bird Cleaning

The quickest and easiest way to clean a game bird involves taking the whole skin and exterior off.

There are just a couple of tools you'll need to begin cleaning your birds:

- A sharp knife or heavy duty shears
- Latex gloves (optional)
- Plastic storage bags

Assuming you have these thing handy, you can begin the process of cleaning your birds. Here's the basic process:

1. Put on your latex gloves, especially if you're cleaning the birds for someone else. It's a good idea to wear gloves to prevent the spread of bacteria. It also helps keep your hands clean of blood and guts as you're cleaning, which is helpful if you have a lot of birds to clean.

2. Grab your sharp knife or heavy duty shears. Start by removing both wings. If you're using a knife, make sure you are always cutting away from your body so you don't accidentally slice yourself.

3. Next, remove both legs at the knee.

4. You then want to remove the head of the bird by cutting the neck as close to the body as you can get.

5. At this point, you can grab the skin and feathers at the top of the breast and just pull right down. You can then slide the skin off the back and over the legs.

6. Cut the tail feathers off as close to the body as possible. Your bird should now be skinless and (mostly) featherless.

7. Lastly, cut a small slit at the base of the breast. You can then slide two fingers in and remove all of the innards (intestines, heart, lungs).

8. Clean your bird up. Pluck any stray feathers that remain. Make sure to get any pellets out of your bird. There's nothing worse than taking a bite of some game bird and almost cracking a tooth on some of the lead shot still left in the bird. Rinse your bird off to get any remaining blood and guts off. Make sure you dry your bird thoroughly before packing it into any plastic storage bags.

From there, it's your choice if you want to leave your bird whole or if you want to further butcher it down to just the parts you want. Some people don't eat the legs and just remove those. Some people breast out the bird so it's just meat and no bones or carcass. It's entirely up to you how you want to do it.

The "It's a Snap" Technique for Cleaning Pheasant and Other Large Upland Game Bird

This is so easy and will save you so much time, I expect fan mail thanking me for introducing you to this technique (as skeptical as you were). Here goes:

1. Place your bird on the ground with its belly up and head pointed away from you.

2. Stand on the bird's wings at the shoulder.

3. Bend over and grab the bird by the legs, using one hand for each leg.

4. Gradually pull up and away from your body. You'll feel the skin and innards releasing.

5. Once you feel that skin releasing, you can do a controlled "snap" up towards your chest and voila! You've skinned and gutted your bird in less than thirty seconds. The legs, neck, innards, and backbone are in your hands and the nice usable breast meat is on the ground.

6. The only thing left is to cut the wings off with your knife or shears and twist the head off the body, and you're done!

This technique works especially well in the field if you're camping and don't want to fuss too much over cleaning your bird.

If you have a particularly plump bird, you can still take the legs off and have a nice little drumstick to gnaw on if you're so inclined.

This technique works great on all of the larger kinds of upland bird like pheasant, chukar, and grouse and makes cleaning your birds a breeze!

Skin in the Game

If you're like me and think that chicken and poultry skin should be its own food group, then you'll want to know how to pluck your birds so you can roast up that bird and get a nice crispy skin on the outside.

There are two ways you can pluck your bird: dry or wet.

1. Dry Plucking

Dry plucking is pretty self-explanatory. You basically sit down with the bird and start plucking away. It's easy yet time consuming and results in a good-looking bird.

The only thing you need to be mindful of is that pheasant and quail have extremely thin skin so you need to pluck carefully and only do one or two feathers at a time so you avoid tearing the skin.

This is a great method if you only have one or two birds to pluck.

2. Wet Plucking

This is a good technique if you've got several birds you want to pluck. You basically scald the bird before plucking and that makes it easier to pluck the feathers off.

Heat up a pot of water to hot but not boiling, around 150 degrees F.

While you're waiting on the water to heat up, pluck the long tail feathers from your pheasant or quail. Once you're done with that, grab the bird by the neck or legs and dunk it into the steaming water for thirty seconds. Pull it out and let it drip dry momentarily. Repeat the process two more times so your bird will have spent a total of ninety seconds in the hot water bath.

Only do one bird at a time as it must remain warm for this technique to work.

Start plucking the warm bird at the wings, working your way toward the long feathers at the breast. Make sure to work quickly but carefully as the skin can tear easily. Only pluck one or two feathers at a time.

From there, work on the flank feathers on the bird's thigh, then the neck, back, and rest of the legs.

Take special care with the quill feathers, the ones with the stiff core, as they are the ones more likely to tear the skin if you pluck them wrong. Pluck the quill in the direction it's pointing and then you might also have to bend it back the other way to finally work the tip out.

And voila! You now have a whole tasty bird that's ready to be roasted, smoked, or put on a rotisserie, delicious skin and all!

Let's eat!

No matter which method you use to clean your birds, the most important part is what you do with them next.

COOK IT

Fabulous Field Chicken Recipes You'll Swear By

You've killed them, you've cleaned them, and now you want to eat them. What do you do with them now?

The good thing with most upland game birds is that you can treat it like a smaller version of chicken. Almost anything you can do with a chicken, you can do with a pheasant or quail. That being said, there are differences in how you will prepare and cook them.

Both birds are smaller than a chicken, so cooking times will automatically be less. Not only is a store-bought frozen chicken going to be bigger, oftentimes it will have been pumped up with fillers like sodium and water. This makes for a juicier breast or piece of meat as well.

Bigger…meatier…juicier…all of this is just to say that a store-bought chicken is going to take a lot more time to cook than any wild bird you harvest. While they might have similar flavor profiles and are largely interchangeable in recipes, preparation times will be markedly different.

And, as with all game meats, *you do not want to overcook it* (I gather you must be sensing a theme by this point in the book).

Fool Proof Ways to Make Moist, Delicious Game Bird Every Time

There are a few different techniques you can use to liven up your bird. It's important to remember with wild game you're dealing with lean meat. That means there's not a lot of fat on the birds, which is what helps give it a nice savory flavor and keeps it tender and juicy.

During the cooking process, you're going to need to add some of that fat and flavor back into the mix. You can accomplish that a few different ways:

Marinades

Once you've cleaned, washed, and let your birds dry thoroughly, you can then proceed to put them in a marinade. When they are in a marinade, they can be used in a matter of hours or frozen and kept for a few months.

I like to make a big batch of marinade that I can use that same day and then have extra to put in a plastic bag with the birds to freeze for future use. Here are a few of my favorite marinades*:

*Quantities listed are for a single serving/quart-sized plastic bag. Adjust as needed for multiple birds. In my experience, it's hard to overdo it on the marinade.

Cilantro-Lime

- 1 tbsp. olive oil
- 1 tbsp. lime juice
- 2 tsp. honey
- 1/4 cup cilantro leaves, chopped
- 1 clove garlic, minced
- 1/8 tsp. salt

Caribbean Jerk

- 1/2 tsp. dried thyme leaves
- 1/2 tsp. ground allspice
- 1 tbsp. brown sugar
- 1/4 tsp. salt
- 1/4 tsp. pepper
- 1/4 tbsp. garlic powder
- 1/4 tsp. cinnamon
- 1/8 tsp. cayenne
- 1 tbsp. olive oil
- 1 tbsp. lime juice

Yogurt-Curry

- 2 tbsp. yogurt
- 1 tsp. lime juice
- 1/8 tsp. salt
- 1 tsp. curry powder
- 1/2 tsp. brown sugar

All of the marinades will pair nicely with some rice and a vegetable of your choice. You can cook the birds a few different ways: in the oven, on the grill, or in a sauté pan if it's just the breast. If you have a whole bird, you can easily butterfly it by cutting out the backbone. This allows the bird to lay flat and then it will cook more easily on a grill or skillet.

Bacon Makes Everything Better

Another way you can impart some flavor and add some fat back into your game bird is by wrapping the breast, or the whole bird, in bacon.

Yes, bacon makes everything better, but we already knew that, didn't we?

Whether it's just wrapping the breast in bacon and grilling it or covering a whole bird and roasting it, using bacon to butter up your birds is a winning idea.

Bacon-wrapped Jalapeno-Cheddar Quail Skewers

• Jalapeno
• Bacon, par-cooked in the microwave for 2 - 4 minutes (less time for less bacon)
• Boneless quail breast, split
• Salt
• Shredded cheddar cheese

Instructions:

1. Pre-heat grill to medium high heat.

2. Cut jalapeño into strips, enough for each split quail breast.

3. Cut bacon slices in half, enough for one half slice per split quail breast.

4. For quail: season each breast with salt. Put one slice of jalapeño on the breast along with some shredded cheese. Fold breast over then wrap with 1/2 piece of bacon. Secure with a skewer. Two breasts can fit on one skewer.

5. Place on grill for 10 minutes or until quail is fully cooked.

6. It's important to note in this recipe the use of par-cooked (partially cooked) bacon. This ensures that you don't overcook the quail while waiting for the bacon to crisp up on the grill.

You'll see many recipes encouraging you to use plain, uncooked bacon and then to grill it for 20 minutes. To me, 20 minutes on direct heat runs too high of a risk of overcooking the quail, making it tough instead of tender. I prefer this method.

Worst case scenario, the quail isn't quite done and you put it back on the grill for a few more minutes. Even if it take 13-14 minutes, you have a perfectly cooked bird that would have been way overcooked at 20 minutes.

You can always bring a bird up to temperature, but you can never salvage a bird that was overcooked.

Sweet Chili Bacon-wrapped Pheasant

- 4 boneless pheasant breasts, split (8 halves)
- 8 slices of bacon
- 1 tbsp. chili powder
- 1 tsp. paprika
- 1/2 tsp. garlic powder
- Salt and pepper
- 1/2 cup brown sugar
- optional: 1/4 tsp. cayenne pepper (for a kick)

Instructions:

1. Preheat oven to 400 degrees.

2. Combine chili powder, garlic, and paprika in a bowl.

3. Roll pheasant breast in spices to coat.

4. Wrap bacon piece around the pheasant breast and put in baking dish.

5. Do for all breast pieces. Once in baking dish, sprinkle tops with brown sugar.

6. Bake for 20-25 minutes.

7. Serve with preferred sides.

Bacon-wrapped Grilled Quail with Orange Maple Glaze

- Bone-in quail breast
- Bacon
- Salt and pepper to taste
- Dried rosemary

Glaze

- 1 cup of orange juice
- 1 cup dry white wine
- 1/2 cup maple syrup (real maple syrup if possible)
- Pinch red pepper flakes

Instructions

1. In a saucepan over medium heat, combine orange juice and wine, and bring to a low boil, stirring frequently, until reduced by half and thick enough to coat the back of a spoon.

2. Add the maple syrup and red pepper flakes and mix.

3. Reduce heat to low while quail cooks.

4. Season each breast with salt, pepper, and rosemary.

5. Wrap each breast with a slice of bacon and secure with a toothpick.

6. Grill 8-10 minutes per side.

7. Halfway through grilling, brush one side of the quail with glaze. Turn over and baste other side of quail with glaze.

8. Turn over once more to set the glaze.

9. Serve hot off the grill.

You'll note that on this recipe it's okay to grill for almost a full 20 minutes. Why is that, you ask? Because of the bone. The bone absorbs the heat before the rest of the bird, which increases overall cooking time.

Surely you've cooked a bone-in steak or pork chop before. If so, you know that a 14 oz. bone-in ribeye takes longer to cook than a 14 oz. center cut ribeye. The same is true for any bone in piece of meat.

Haley's Favorite Upland Bird Recipe

The last recipe I want to share is one of my favorite appetizers. This one is a good one if you only have one or two birds and it's not enough to make a meal out of them. You'll impress the heck out of your friends if you serve this before the main course comes out.

Quail and Sun-dried Tomato Flatbread with Carrot Top Pesto

- Breast of 1 or 2 quail
- Olive oil
- Salt and pepper
- 1/2 cup julienned sun-dried tomato
- Shredded mozzarella cheese
- 1/2 teaspoon Italian seasoning
- 1 sheet frozen puff pastry
- 2 tbsp. flour
- Carrot top pesto (recipe below)

Carrot Top Pesto

- 1 cup lightly packed carrot leaves, stems removed
- 6 tbsp. extra virgin olive oil
- 1 large garlic clove
- 1/4 tsp. salt
- 3 tbsp. pine nuts, toasted
- 1/4 cup freshly grated parmesan cheese

Instructions:

1. Pull out sheet of puff pastry and let defrost according to package directions.

2. Once defrosted, unfold pastry sheet onto a lightly floured surface.

3. Use a rolling pin to gently roll out dough into a rectangular shape.

4. Once dough is to your desired shape and size, put it on a baking sheet lined with parchment paper.

5. Start making carrot top pesto. Combine carrot leaves, oil, garlic, pine nuts, and salt in a food processor or blender and process until smooth. Add the parmesan and pulse just until blended.

6. Slice quail breast into medallions. Season lightly with salt and pepper.

7. Heat olive oil over medium heat. Sauté quail breasts in oil 3-4 minutes just until there's no pink left in the middle.

8. Spread pesto over the puff pastry.

9. Top with quail medallions, sun-dried tomato, and mozzarella cheese. Sprinkle Italian seasoning on top.

10. Bake in a preheated oven at 400 degrees for 20 minutes or until the crust is golden brown.

11. Serve and enjoy! Guests will be impressed!

I had pulled some carrots from out of my garden and was wondering what I could do with those beautiful carrot tops as it seemed such a waste to just throw them out. That's when I came across the recipe for a yummy looking pesto that I adapted to use carrot tops rather than arugula. From there I conceived of the rest of the dish and we were all stunned at how amazing it tasted.

If you have leftover pesto, it goes well on some fresh baked bread smothered in butter. I was downing the stuff the next day and couldn't get enough of it. You can also use it in other recipes, but it should be used up within a matter of days as it won't keep after that.

Of course, if you can't make carrot top pesto, then the recipe will be just as delicious with regular pesto as well.

Cook On!

Hopefully you've gotten some good ideas from these recipes and thought of new ways to cook your birds that you hadn't thought of before.

Don't be shy about experimenting with different ways of cooking your game birds. You'll eventually find one or two surefire ways that you'll rely on that will please your family and impress your guests.

Chapter Four

TURKEY

HUNT IT

Killer Cures for Longbeard Fever

Every year in the spring between the months of February until May, a weird illness spreads throughout many states in the U.S. The illness causes temporary paralysis whereby one sits motionless for hours on end. It can also cause an unhealthy obsession with beards, a slight foot fetish, and a delirium that results in imperviousness to dangerous reptiles and insects surrounding a person.

The fever goes by several names but the most common ones are gobbler fever, tom fever, and longbeard fever.

I am, of course, referring to spring turkey season whereby many hunters abandon all reason to sit motionless in the woods for hours at a time in the hopes of luring a boss tom with an 11-inch beard and 2-inch spurs right into their welcoming arms all the while pretending not to notice the swarm of mosquitos feasting on their flesh and the occasional cottonmouth in their path.

Turkey hunting can be simultaneously exhilarating and yet frustratingly devoid of action. One must wait hours on end with virtually no activity and with patience wearing thin but all of a sudden and without warning be richly rewarded with a fantastic finish of a prize gobbler or two finally strutting into view.

The endless wait becomes worth it when the tom finally stops strutting long enough to lift his head into view and BAM! You've got him!

To the outside observer, turkey hunting may appear to be a lot of hurry up and wait. While this is true to some extent, there's a lot of action that's taking place and a subtle *pas de deux* between hunter and gobbler that might not be apparent to the casual observer.

We'll find out more about this delicate dance and techniques to increase your chances of bagging that boss tom as we delve into this chapter.

Five of a Kind

There are five subspecies of wild turkey in the United States. They are:

- Eastern wild turkey

- Osceola

- Rio Grande

- Merriam's

- Gould's

Eastern Wild Turkeys

Eastern wild turkeys are widely distributed throughout the U.S. While they are most common east of the Mississippi, they can be found in thirty-eight states throughout the U.S. and are the most common species overall.

They are the strongest gobblers and have the longest beards of all the subspecies. They are the second most difficult to call in after the Osceola.

Osceolas

These are also known as Florida wild turkey as these guys are located exclusively in Florida.

This is one of the most prized turkey species because they are known to be the most difficult to call in. They also boast the longest spurs, albeit slightly shorter beards than Eastern wild turkey.

Rio Grande

Rio Grande turkeys, unsurprisingly, are found all throughout Texas as well as other desert regions like Oklahoma, Kansas, and even parts of Mexico.

Many hunters will flock to Texas in the spring to get their cure for tom fever. Rio Grande turkeys are middle of the pack in terms of beard length, spur length, and gobbling ability.

Merriam's

These are going to be your mountainous turkeys, particularly concentrated in the Rocky Mountain regions.

While they make a nice source of food for locals to those regions, they are not a highly sought after species due to having the shortest beard, shortest spurs, and weakest gobbles of the species.

Gould's

These are the least numerous of all the species of turkey. They are only found in New Mexico, Arizona, and northern Mexico.

Similar to the Rio Grandes, they are moderate in beard, spur, and gobbles.

The Proper Chokes for Your Gobbler

As you may know, chokes are a way of modifying your pattern and range from a shotgun without having to buy a different gun for each different type of game. Choke sizes range from the very open skeet or cylinder with virtually no constriction to super-full chokes with the tightest constriction and densest patterns.

Whereas you might use a more open modified or improved cylinder to bag waterfowl and other upland bird varieties, the special nature of turkey shooting requires a tighter choke. This is anything from a full choke to an actual specific turkey choke. The benefit of a tighter choke is sufficient pattern density at longer distances. Using an extra-full or turkey choke allows you enough pattern density to put down a bird even as far out as fifty yards.

Unlike with most other game varieties, with turkey you're going to be aiming for the neck and head. This is a much smaller target than the typical body shot where you're aiming for vital organs. A body shot on a heavily feathered and heavily muscled gobbler might cripple the bird but still allow it to get away. The safest, most ethical shot for a turkey is a neck and head shot.

Many hunters can make do with only a full choke if they know they'll be making more close-range shots inside thirty yards. In those circumstances, an extra full or turkey choke might be too tight and cause misses at closer range because the pattern is only the size of a baseball at the twenty yard range. Your aim has to be spot on at that short range to make a kill shot with a super-full or turkey choke.

This is where it's important to know your territory and your bird. The notoriously difficult to call in Osceolas might only offer you longer range shots where a super-full choke will be necessary. The less wary Merriam's, however, might only require a full choke because you can typically shoot them at shorter distances than other turkey varieties.

Loads and Chokes

Of course, the choke size is only one piece of the puzzle when it comes to ghosting gobblers. Load size is also a huge consideration in this equation. Depending on your gun and shell size, the standard shot for turkey is going to be anywhere from #4s to #7s, with most people settling on #5s or #6s. If you really can't decide, some manufacturers even have shells with mixed loads in there, blending a range of #5s, #6s, and #7s into the shot to cover all your bases no matter how far away your target is.

Geez, with so many possible choke/load combinations, how does one even begin to choose?

Pattern, pattern, and pattern some more.

Something that any serious hunter needs to be doing with all their guns regularly in the off season is target practice, patterning, sighting in, and experimenting with various types of ammo at varying distances. You can't hang your gun up for months on end and then expect to pick it up again a day or two before season and wonder why you keep missing your prized game.

Patterning for turkey can be slightly different than patterning for other types of game birds. When patterning on a turkey silhouette you want to see a good number of pellets hitting the head and neck area. This indicates your spread at that range is sufficient for a kill shot.

One of the more deceptive patterns is the neck shot. On paper, it looks like you've decapitated the bird with the hole you've blown out in the neck area. While it looks good on paper, this isn't an ideal pattern for real life. It's too dense for a small turkey head that's constantly bobbing and weaving, leaving too little margin for error.

That's why you want to see a nice array of pellets hitting both the neck and head area. If too few pellets hit that key area and if your spread is too wide—you won't have enough pellets on target to make regular kill shots. Too dense, however, like one giant blown out hole in your target, and your pattern leaves too little margin for error if your aim is off or if the turkey moves its head at the last second.

Ideally, you're looking for seventy percent of your shot in a thirty-inch circle at forty yards for a full choke shot. More open chokes will be less dense at that range. Only around sixty percent of your shot will make it in the circle with a modified choke, and even less the more open you go.

No matter what you're patterning for, be sure to mark each target with the load, ammo, distance, gun, and choke you're using as you test each one. Compare the targets side by side to see which combination patterns best.

Doing it with some buddies can help cut down on ammo expenses as well as you can each try some of the other's load and choke combos. You only need a few shots with each combo to see what works and what doesn't.

Find the Roost to Get the Boost

Despite being technically classified as an upland bird, turkey hunting is more akin to waterfowl hunting.

The first similarity is the need for thorough scouting before the hunt to identify probable areas your gobblers will be frequenting. Try to find where the gobblers are roosting at night so you can position yourself on the ground nearby in the morning waiting for them to fly down.

What does turkey scouting entail, exactly?

First and foremost, you need to make sure there are actually turkeys in the area where you plan to hunt. Just because you saw a flock somewhere in December doesn't mean that's where they're going to be in April. The good news is that turkey tend to stay within a relatively small radius of around forty miles. I say small because they don't travel too far from day to day, perhaps seven miles or so within this radius.

The best way to scout is to look for turkey signs. The telltale three-toed turkey tracks are easy to spot. Droppings, feathers, and scratch marks from where they've been digging for insects are also sure signs you're on the right track.

Another good sign to look for is long, straight lines in the dirt. Sometimes with turkey tracks it might be ambiguous as to whether they're hens or gobblers. Long lines in the dirt confirm the presence of gobblers—those drag marks are made when a gobbler is dragging his wing tips while strutting around.

Just as important as seeing turkey tracks is hearing them. A good part of turkey hunting requires listening since calling and communication is such an integral part of the hunt. Stopping to listen for gobblers is of particular importance when you're trying to identify the roost. Good times to do this are in the evening or first thing in the morning. Gobblers are most vocal first thing in the morning just before they fly down, so heading out a day or two before opening day before daybreak to listen out for where the birds are roosting is a good idea. Identifying the roost will give you a huge advantage and significantly boost your odds of being able to win the affection of that tom you've been tracking all this time.

When you do identify the roost or other likely locations your turkeys will be heading toward, it's time to strategize. Pick out the shooting lanes you want to lure your toms to while staying well concealed. If you're using decoys, visualize where you'll be setting these up in relation to your blind/tree and the likely direction they'll be coming from.

Preparation is key to any successful hunting endeavor. Spending some time to stop, look, and listen in the days and weeks before opening day will go a long way toward boosting the odds you bag that boss tom you've been longing for.

The Call of the Wild Turkey

Another way turkey hunting is closer to waterfowl hunting than other upland bird hunting is through the use of calls. Calling is essential to turkey hunting, perhaps even more so than in waterfowling.

Waterfowl have an aerial view of the landscape. They might hone in on your decoy spread without you ever having to make a peep on your call. This only happens a fraction of the time, but it does happen.

With turkey hunting, this isn't the case. They're on the ground, not flying in the air. Even with decoys, they aren't necessarily drawn in because of the decoy set up itself but rather because you lured them in with a series of irresistible clucks and yelps. Only then do they discover your decoys.

What makes turkey hunting so frustrating yet exhilarating at the same time is that you're trying to get a tom to act against his nature. With a real hen, the tom can just gobble away and strut his stuff and an interested hen will go to him.

You're trying get the gobbler to come to you. He wants to hang out and wait for the hen to be lured by his irresistible charm and you need to override his willful pride by somehow getting him to come to you, or at least meet you halfway. The only way you're going to do that is by calling.

Let's dive in a bit deeper to explore one of the most essential parts of the turkey hunt.

A Symphony of Sounds

There are four kinds of calls commonly used in turkey hunting. It doesn't hurt to have more than one style of call on you at all times. Not only do turkeys respond to the type of call being made (cutt, yelp, cluck, etc.), but they will also respond to a variance in pitch that can be created from changing up the type of call you're using. If you're not getting any response whatsoever, try your locator call to see if you can elicit a shock gobble from a tom and pinpoint his location.

Box Call

A box call consists of a long, rectangular hollow box—typically a wooden one, although they've been making synthetic waterproof ones recently—with a thin paddle over top of it. The paddle is pegged to the top end of the box and pivots from side to side over the lip of the box.

When you scrape the bottom side of the paddle against the lip of the box, you can make various turkey noises that reverberate through the box and project it outward.

Slate Call

A slate call is a two-piece call consisting of a striker and a palm sized cylinder roughly one inch tall. The cylinder has a striking surface on the top side and holes drilled out on the bottom side to create an echo chamber that can be heard some distance away.

To use, you grasp your striker like a pencil and scrape the tip of it along the surface of the pot. Varying your stroke creates the various sounds a turkey makes.

Mouth or Diaphragm Call

This one is fairly self-explanatory, but it's a call that you place in your mouth. Think of it like a flat, two-dimensional mouth guard with a similar U-shape designed to fit in your mouth. The call has reeds that you blow air across by mimicking certain words to make turkey sounds.

The benefit of a mouth call is that it allows for hands-free operation. You can make calls with it while readying your gun to shoot or crawling around searching for cover.

The downside is that there is a steeper learning curve with this call versus the others. If you're already proficient with duck or goose calls, it might not be as challenging. If you're a novice to all calls, you might be better off starting with a box or slate call.

Locator Calls

Turkeys are known to do what's called a "shock gobble." This is an instinctive or reflexive noise that turkeys make in reaction to another noise they hear. A locator call is intended to elicit a shock gobble from a turkey for the purposes of locating the flock or the gobbler in question.

Locator calls are typically calls from an entirely different animal, often a crow or owl. Duck, goose, coyote, and hawk calls work as well though. You don't want to use this call repeatedly, just sparingly enough to get the reaction you're looking for and hone in on your target.

Talk Turkey to Me—Calling Strategies to Lure in Stubborn Toms

Now that you have your turkey orchestra tucked away in your pocket, it's time to learn how to use it.

You have to learn to become the Turkey Whisperer. You're communicating with the turkey and have to know how to respond to the sounds you're hearing—or not hearing—to ultimately lure that gobbler in your direction. This is when the dance begins, the *pas de deux* I mentioned at the beginning of the chapter.

The two most basic calls you must master right away to just get you started are the plain cluck and the hen yelp.

If you want to level up, however, you'll need to add more calls to your arsenal. Other good ones to add are tree yelps, fly down cackles, cutting, purrs, and the kee-kee sound of young jakes.

Once you've got those mastered, here are a few strategies for how to talk so a turkey will listen and listen so a turkey will talk:

Miss Sassy Pants Strategy

This is a great strategy to use early- to mid-season when a lot of gobblers are "henned up." This is when a gobbler is already surrounded by so many hens that there's no feasible reason why he should even think of coming your direction.

Even with hens, there's a clear pecking order and hierarchy amongst them. If you pay attention, you should be able to see or hear the boss hen. She's usually the loudest, the one that sasses the other hens to keep them in their place, and the one the other hens follow. She doesn't like it when another hen starts sassing back. This is what you'll be doing. Imitate her every sound. If she yelps, you yelp. If she cutts, you cutt.

The goal is to get her so worked up about another Miss Sassy Pants in the area that she'll come investigate. If she does so, you can be sure the toms will follow. That's when you'll have your chance at your longbeard.

New Tom on the Block Strategy

This is a good strategy to use on a hung-up tom. You've done most of the leg work and gotten a tom to approach, but he's just out of shooting range, and no amount of plaintive hen calling will get him to come any closer.

This is because he's waiting for that plaintive hen to come to him. He's off in the distance strutting his stuff thinking that the hen that's been yearning for him for the past couple hours is finally going to make her move.

At this point in time, you've won the battle but lost the war, so to speak. This is when you should switch up your call. Instead of making another hen yelp or cluck, you can make a couple jake yelps instead. These have the same cadence as a hen yelp but are longer and deeper.

A jake yelp is going to seriously tick off that boss tom that's been strutting his stuff in the distance. He won't be able to stand the thought of some young whippersnapper marching in on his territory and getting close to that hen that was supposed to saunter his way any minute now. He might be so mad he'll finally have to come in closer to fight off that jake trying to steal his girl.

This works especially well if you have a jake decoy you're using to make the scenario more real. It gets extra exciting when the tom starts beating up on the jake decoy itself!

The Silent Treatment Strategy

Sometimes silence can be just as deadly as the turkey orchestra in your pocket.

For whatever reason, some days gobblers have a serious case of "shut mouth" disease. This is when they are just not being responsive to any of your calls even though you know they're out there. These are the days when a hunter can get busted big time. They're too busy making calls that they weren't ready for the silent approach of the tom and get busted.

On these days, you need to match their mood and shut your own mouth. More calling isn't going to do the job. It's a job for Job instead, meaning patience, patience, patience. Use your call sparingly, just enough to let a tom know you're there, but sometimes not even calling back if you do hear a gobble.

Let his curiosity get the better of him. When you give him the silent treatment, he might think that hen he was hearing is leaving the area and might decide to pursue her. When he does, you'll be ready. Your call will be tucked away and you won't get busted by a silent approach that you weren't expecting.

There are many more strategies you can employ with your calling. The more calls you've mastered, the more tricks you have up your sleeve.

There's nothing more satisfying than spending a few hours verbally dancing back and forth with a big gobbler and finally convincing him that where you are is where he wants to be. That's when you know you've mastered the art of talking turkey.

The Art of the Decoy—Winning Decoy Strategies to Seal the Deal

Here again we have another similarity between waterfowl hunting and turkey hunting, and that's with the use of decoys. Thankfully, you don't need nearly as many decoys with turkey hunting as you do with duck or goose hunting—just a few will do.

Once you've gotten the attention of a gobbler or two with the sweet, sweet sound of your calling, having a good decoy set up will seal the deal. Unlike in waterfowling, a decoy spread in turkey hunting isn't mandatory. It's more like icing on the cake.

A decoy set-up is for hunters who are going about it more old-style with the "sit and wait" method to turkey hunting. Those who prefer the more modern "run and gun" style of hunting are on the move too much to make use of decoy set up.

Neither style is right or wrong. You just have to know when to use each one.

If you're planning on using the "sit and wait" strategy, whether in a pop-up blind or just hidden away behind a tree trunk, using a good decoy set-up can be just the thing you need to seal the deal with that gobbler you've been tracking for days or weeks on end.

Here are some proven decoy tips and strategies to help you ghost your gobbler:

Close Counts

You want your spread to be fairly close to where you'll be hiding, ten to twenty yards out. This is in case a gobbler gets hung up and doesn't want to fully commit, he still might be in range for an ethical shot.

Be Visible

Decoy set-ups in fields where you're hidden just inside the tree line tend to work well. The toms can spot the decoys from a distance, hear your calls, and will be inclined to make an approach. Gobblers are less wary if they can spot the decoys well in advance.

Conversely, if you're hunting in heavily wooded areas, decoys might not be necessary or effective if they won't be seen until it's too late.

Be Invisible

While you want your decoys to be very visible, you yourself want to stay invisible. That means setting up your decoys to the side of your position, not directly in front of your position.

If you're positioned directly in the line of sight of your decoy, any movement you make to raise your gun or shift positions leaves you at risk of the turkey busting you and scaring off.

Strategically position your decoys just enough to the side that the tom will be focused on the decoy and not notice you.

The Submissive Hen

This is a hen that's ready to breed. Lustful gobblers won't be able to stay away. If you pair this with a jake decoy in the background, it will be particularly effective, especially to older gobblers and boss toms higher up in the pecking order who aren't about to let that jake beat them to the hen.

If you set the submissive hen up directly on the ground without a stake, this can drive the toms wild as they try and mount it and she's rolling over and playing hard to get.

The Gobbler Decoy

Some hunters shy away from using a gobbler decoy or full-strut decoy. They may scare away or intimidate jakes or more subordinate toms. This can be a mistake, though, especially in early season.

If you've got another boss tom in the field and he's already itching for a fight because he's henless, seeing that gobbler decoy is going to draw him right in because he's ready to whoop butt.

The gobbler decoy can even work for subordinate toms and jakes. These guys sometimes just want to act like a wingman for the boss tom knowing that boss tom is going to be bringing in the ladies. He'll probably get some action by default and wants to buddy up with him.

Either way, with a gobbler decoy, you can get a tom to *commit* rather than getting hung up in the distance like he can with hens.

The Jake Decoy

This is a good one to use later in the season. It's less intimidating than a gobbler or full strut decoy. Often, by late season, subordinate toms have gotten beat up enough by boss toms that they're wary of approaching another strutting tom. But a little jake that they can buddy up with or even go beat up on might be just what they need late in the season as they get desperate to breed.

I Have a Fever and the Only Cure is MORE LONGBEARDS!

If you find yourself infected with longbeard fever each spring, the tips, tricks, and strategies I've presented above will go a long way toward treating you. Unfortunately, there is no known permanent cure for longbeard fever. It's an ailment that many a hunter lives with their whole lives.

Sometimes, the disease evolves and morphs into similar mutations like quack fever, elk fever, or buck fever. Whichever kind of fever you become afflicted with, the best thing to do is just let it run its course.

Following all of the techniques, strategies, and tips presented in this book will help shorten the fever, no matter which one you happen to be afflicted with. Just be ready for it to hit you again next season!

CLEAN IT

From Tom to Table—Clean It, Skin It, Pluck It, Eat It

Once you've cleaned one bird, you've cleaned 'em all! This is more or less true when it comes to upland bird and waterfowl hunting.

There are a couple more tricks you can use when it comes to cleaning ducks and geese that will make life a lot easier for you, and you'll learn about those in the upcoming chapters. Cleaning a turkey is a pretty straightforward process that's not much different from cleaning a pheasant, chukkar, grouse, chicken, or any other kind of game bird, wild or domestic.

Let's do a refresher course on how to clean your wild turkeys like a boss!

It Starts in the Field

There's not much field care required for wild turkey. If you're going straight home after the hunt, you can get away with just slinging your bird over your shoulder and dealing with it once you get home.

If you happen to be hunting in warmer climates or closer to summer, there are a couple steps you can take to ensure your bird stays clean and safe.

Keep dirt and debris off your bird

Any dirt, leaves, needles, or grass that are sticking to your bird, especially around the wound, should be promptly cleaned off. Once this is done, make sure to keep your bird off the ground from here on out. Sling it over your shoulder or use a rope or other carrier to transport your bird. *Do not drag it on the ground behind you.*

Beware the blood

Captain Obvious says: "Blood is sticky." This should be a consideration as to whether you go ahead and gut and/or remove any appendages in the field, but not fully clean it. Not only will dirt and debris be more likely to stick, but the feathers will too. Having feathers sticking to your meat while you're trying to clean it makes the process substantially longer.

If you'll be stuck in the field for quite some time in warm weather, I'd recommend gutting it on the spot. It's harder to clean a pre-gutted bird no matter if you'll be skinning or plucking it, but if you have no choice, clean it in the field.

Pluck or Skin?

As with any game bird, one must make the decision as to whether to pluck or to skin the bird. Plucking takes quite a bit longer than skinning, but the results are worth it. You have a beautiful bird fit for roasting. Plus, you have peace of mind that you will use the entire bird and not waste anything.

Unlike with other upland bird or waterfowl, you typically only have one turkey to deal with. Even though plucking might take a bit longer, at least you only have to do one of them. If you've got a hill of quail or your limit of ducks staring at you, plucking a bunch of those suckers becomes significantly less appealing (although you should still strive to do it every so often).

I discussed in the quail and pheasant section the two ways to pluck a bird: wet plucking or dry plucking.

The methods hold true for turkey just as much as they do for quail and pheasant, so you can refer back to that chapter if you need a refresher. It will most likely be easier to employ the wet plucking technique for turkey due to the size of the bird.

Be Roast Turkey Ready in Five Easy Steps

You opted to pluck your bird so you can put a beautiful roast turkey on your table—hooray!

I know plucking the bird was hard work, but you're not quite done yet. Now you have to clean and gut your bird.

But have no fear! This part can be done in just five easy steps.

1. Remove the oil gland

To be honest, this step is optional. Most of the time, the tiny gland isn't going to release enough oil to seriously mess with your meat. If you're the "better safe than sorry" type, remove it.

Place the turkey on its breast. The oil gland is located at the base of the back just above where the tail connects. It's only about the size of a marble, but you can cut it out using shears or a sharp paring knife.

2. Remove the appendages

If you haven't already done so, remove the head and the feet. The feet can be removed at the ankles where feather meets scale. You'll also want to go ahead and chop off the wing tips at the last joint as well. You can use heavy duty shears or a sharp butcher's cleaver for any of these parts.

3. Remove the windpipe and craw

Turn the turkey on its back. Cut away the membrane that connects the neck and breast bone if it's still intact. Be very careful not to puncture the craw that sits in the chest cavity. The trachea and esophagus are easily removed once the skin is cut away from the neck. Reach in and gently pull the craw out. Do this by working your fingers in between the craw and skin on the chest.

4. Remove the innards

Make a shallow, skin-deep incision around the circumference of the anus. You don't want to cut into the intestines. Then make a small slit in the skin on the abdomen just below the anus. Slowly and gently pull the intestines out to prevent rupturing them. Reach in the cavity and pull out the organs.

You can keep the organs to cook separately. Make sure to gently remove the green bile sac from the liver. Cut open the gizzard and remove the yellow lining. Pull out the heart from deep inside the body cavity. Lastly will be the lungs, which can be tricky to remove the first time. They're tucked firmly against the rib cage. Discard the lungs.

5. Rinse thoroughly

The hard work is done! Now just rinse out the inside and the outside of your bird, making sure to remove any blood clots, feces, or any other debris on the inside or outside of the bird.

This is also a good time to pluck any remaining stubborn feathers, cut out bloodshot meat, and remove any shot from the meat. Dry it thoroughly before roasting or seal, freeze, and save for later.

Skin Off, Breasts Out!

Woo-hoo, it's party time! Oh wait, we're talking about turkeys, not Mardi Gras? My bad.

Well, we can still have some fun skinning and breasting out our gobbler.

This is typically the easiest way to clean a turkey. It can be done in the field or at home, and it's the same process you'll use when skinning and breasting out your duck or goose.

The only difference and the reason I want to cover it here as well is because, when skinning and breasting out a turkey, you do have to mind the craw.

Here's the process you'll go through to skin and breast out your turkey:

1. Remove the beard and fan if you want to save those items

You can cut or simply twist off the beard from the front chest of the bird. To cut off the fan, hold the tail feathers and locate the anus. Cut right above the anus from behind and remove the tail feathers. Doing it this way allows you to keep some of the secondary feathers if you were plan on doing a mount.

2. Show us your—never mind!

It's time to expose the breast area. All you have to do is make a small, vertical incision on the skin of the turkey on the front side. From there, grab on both sides and pull it open. Remove the skin and feathers from the meat as far down as you can to expose as much breast as possible. You might have to use a sharp knife to remove the skin from the meat in some places.

3. Remove the breast

Using a sharp knife, cut along one side of the breast bone as close as you can, almost as if you were filleting a fish. Filet from top to bottom, carefully removing the breast from the breast bone. Continue on down the sides toward the wings. Repeat on both sides of the breast.

4. Beware the crop (craw)!

As you're cutting away your breast, be mindful of not cutting open the craw. The craw is a sac deep in the turkey's throat where it stores food until it's ready to be digested. If you accidentally slice it open, the grain and other food particles being stored in there will get all over your meat and inside your bird. You can always rinse the particles off your bird, but it just prolongs the cleaning process, not to mention is a rather smelly affair.

You can push the craw out of the way by cutting the skin away at the top of the breast where the breast and chest cavity is. From there, you can gently free the craw from where it rests in the chest cavity by cutting the skin around it. It can then be pushed up and out of the way while you continue breasting out your bird.

6. Don't forget the legs!

Yes, wild turkey legs are edible. I've met a lot of hunters who seem to think turkey legs are inedible. I'll talk more about how to cook them in the next chapter, but first, let's remove them.

They're already partially exposed from pulling back the feathers and skin from the breast. Now, you just skin up the leg using a sharp knife until you reach the scaly part of the leg. Keep pulling the skin and feathers away from the meat as you go. Slice a little, pull a little until you finally reveal the leg and thigh meat.

Once you get to the base of thigh, you'll want to slice the thigh away from the body. Pull the leg down and away from the body to expose the inner thigh area, and you can see where you need to slice.

There you go! It'll be a Mardi Gras in your mouth once you get around to cooking some of the tasty recipes included in the next section.

If you're mindful of waste, you can use the carcass and giblets to make a delicious turkey stock for use in soups and sauces.

Invite Tom Over for Turkey Dinner!

Your bird is prepped and ready for cooking. In the next chapter, you'll learn lots of delicious ways to prepare your turkey. We'll dispel of the myth that wild turkey legs are no good and learn how to make use of the whole turkey when cooking. Before you know it, you'll be ready to invite Tom over to enjoy some tasty tom turkey at the table for twelve!

COOK IT

Tasty Turkey That Will Tantalize the Taste Buds

Wild turkey is easier to cook than one might think, but for some reason people tend to get intimidated by turkey. Maybe it's because it's a larger bird and they're scared of ruining such a large piece of meat, or maybe they just never learned the proper way to cook it.

I've known a lot of hunters who won't even try to shoot a turkey because they claim that the meat is no good. I would beg to differ. Hopefully, with the help of some of these cooking tips and recipes, you'll be more confident about putting some wild turkey on your table.

Brine, Baby, Brine!

The absolute key to moist, delicious, non-gamey turkey is to brine that baby.

What's brining? Good question.

Brining is the act of immersing your meat in a saltwater solution for a period of time before cooking. This adds moisture, tenderness, and flavor to your meat, something particularly helpful to wild game, which is typically leaner and tougher than store-bought meats.

The use of salt helps break down muscle fibers that typically contract during the cooking process, resulting in tough, dried out meat. Merely submerging your meat in a water bath without the salt will not produce the same result.

There are two ways to brine your meat: wet brine and dry brine. Wet brine is the more traditional method. Dry brining has recently gained momentum and is the lesser used, but still very effective, technique. Let's discuss the differences.

Wet Brining

The traditional method of wet brining involves submersing your meat—typically a leaner, dryer cut of meat like chicken, turkey, or pork—in a solution of salt water. The water should have around a six percent salt content to it, which equates to about one cup of salt for every one gallon of water.

You'll need a container that's big enough to fully submerge your meat in. For a large, whole turkey, use a huge stock pot or a cooler to fit the whole turkey in. Make sure to keep your meat cool while it brines, a somewhat difficult task for a large turkey.

There are a couple of solutions, however.

Clear out space in your fridge to fit a stockpot with turkey or use a spare refrigerator.

Fill some 2 liter soda bottles 3/4 of the way with water and freeze. Create your brine bath in a cooler or plastic tub. Add the frozen water bottles to the cooler to keep your brining turkey below 40 degrees. Change out 2 liter bottles periodically while brining to keep mixture cool.

If it's winter, keep cool outside in a covered, protected area.

Typically you'll want to brine your bird for anywhere between 12-36 hours. Additionally, if you've left the skin on your turkey and you want it to crisp up nicely in the oven, you'll want to let your turkey dry thoroughly as well before cooking—at least overnight in the refrigerator or other temperature controlled cool spot.

Some recipes call for the use of aromatics in the brine—herbs, vegetables, and other ingredients that are supposed to impart flavor into the turkey as it brines. Normally I'd be all about those aromatics but I've come across research explaining why they don't do as much apart from make your brine smell good.

Basically, the molecular compounds of the food cells are too large to pass through the fibers of the meat, unlike salt ions which are both small and electrically charged and pass through easily. The aromatics might penetrate the surface of your meat but won't do as much to infuse the whole bird with flavor.

If that bit of extra flavor is worth using up your time and ingredients on, then by all means, add some aromatics to your brine. If you do, make sure to boil your brine first and let it completely cool down before submerging your bird.

Dry Brining

The less common way to brine is known as dry brining. It almost sounds like an oxymoron because the definition of brining is to submerge your food in a salt water solution prior to cooking, but it's not.

Dry brining involves merely just heavily salting your meat and leaving it to sit for 12-36 hours. If you plan on brining your bird for longer than 24 hours, you'll want to loosely cover it with plastic wrap to prevent too much moisture being lost through evaporation.

You'll need roughly half a cup of Kosher salt in a small bowl. If the skin is still on your turkey, you'll also want to add 2 tablespoons of baking powder to the salt. Baking powder will help get the skin extra crispy.

Taking your thumb and forefingers, grab a hefty pinch of salt. Hold 6 to 10 inches above the bird and sprinkle salt all over, allowing for an even coat of salt. The turkey should be well coated but not totally encrusted in salt. You don't have to use the whole amount of salt. In fact, you probably won't. Just use enough to coat your bird thoroughly.

Transfer to a rimmed baking sheet fitted with a rack and refrigerate uncovered for 12-24 hours or longer.

Many people prefer the dry brining method because it helps the turkey retain moisture without watering down the flavor. The end result is a more intensely flavored bird.

That might be fine with a store-bought bird, but with a game bird, you will want to water it down to reduce the gamey taste. Dry brining it on its own may or may not be enough to take away the gaminess. The best thing to do is to experiment the next time you bag a wild turkey and see for yourself which method is better.

Once you've brined those babies, now it's time to cook them!

Turkey: The Original White Meat

Ever since the Pilgrim days, Americans have held the unassuming turkey in high regard. For generations, we've sat around a Thanksgiving table surrounded by family and friends and celebrated our nation's early, difficult days by serving turkey to remind us of the abundance that surrounds us.

If dried out turkey that you have to drown in gravy in order to make it remotely edible has become the tradition in your family, it's time to up your turkey game!

Whole Roasted Thanksgiving Turkey

- 1 10-12 pound wet or dry brined turkey, skin on
- Olive oil*
- Salt and pepper*

*If you've dry-brined your turkey, you don't need to use olive oil or any additional salt or pepper.

Instructions:

1. Preheat oven to 325 degrees.

2. If turkey has been dry-brined, leave as is. If turkey has been wet brined and dried thoroughly, rub a thin layer of olive oil to coat the skin and then sprinkle a generous amount of salt and pepper on the skin.

3. Place turkey breast side up in a shallow roasting pan. Do not add water.

4. Cover turkey with a loose tent of foil to prevent over-browning of skin.

5. Roast approximately 3 hours, removing foil for the last 30 minutes of roasting to allow the skin to get golden and crispy.

6. Do no baste while roasting. It can't penetrate the skin and causes the skin to get soggy while washing away the seasonings on the skin. If properly brined, no basting should be needed.

6. Be sure to use a meat thermometer to gauge temperature. Stick it in fleshy part of the thigh without touching the bone. Once internal temperature of thigh reaches 150 degrees F, remove from oven.

7. Let turkey rest at least 30 minutes before carving to redistribute the juices and keep turkey moist. The temperature will also continue to rise for several minutes after roasting, so you can remove from oven a touch before reaching the 165 degree mark so as to prevent overcooking.

This is just a simple, basic roast turkey recipe. There will be variations in cooking times based on how large your bird is, if the cavity is stuffed or unstuffed, etc. That's why it's important to use a meat thermometer because that will be the most accurate gauge as to whether your turkey is done.

Starting at around the 2 hour mark, I'd start taking the temperature of your bird every 30 minutes or so. Be sure to remember to take the foil tent off once your turkey gets close to being the correct temperature, around the 130 degree mark.

For those who want to stuff their bird with stuffing, it's advisable to at least partially heat it up before you stuff your bird with it. It takes longer to heat up than the bird and you run the risk of it not getting up to a safe temperature before it's time to take the turkey out of the oven.

You can also stuff the cavity of the turkey with aromatics instead of stuffing. This can be a range of things including: garlic, onion wedges, lemon wedges, rosemary sprigs, parsley, apple wedges, carrots, celery, and more. Use your imagination here.

Spatchcocking Method

Spatchcocking is a method where you split open your bird so that it lays flat on the grill or in the oven and cooks more evenly. It's a simple process—just take a sharp knife or some heavy-duty shears and cut the backbone out of the bird. Open it up and lay it flat on your cooking surface, breast side up.

There are a few benefits to spatchcocking birds, especially larger birds like turkey.

First, it ensures even cooking time. The legs will get done at the same time as the breast so you won't end up with dry white meat that you have to drown in sauce or gravy.

Also, it takes up less room in your oven so you can even cook two birds at once or bake a side dish at the same time as you're roasting your bird.

And, perhaps most importantly, it takes about half the time to cook this way versus traditional roasting. What takes around 3 hours for a normal turkey can be done in about 90 minutes by spatchcocking it.

So if you're convinced that spatchcocking a turkey is the best way to prepare it, here's a basic recipe that allows you to do just that.

Spatchcock Roast Turkey

- 1 whole turkey, brined and butterflied
- 2 tbsp. vegetable oil
- Salt and pepper

Instructions:

1. Preheat oven to 450 degrees. Line a rimmed baking sheet or roasting pan with foil and set a broiler rack or wire rack inside.

2. Pat turkey dry with paper towel. Rub skin with oil. Season with salt and pepper. If turkey was dry brined, no need to add any extra salt.

3. Place turkey on rack, pressing down on breast bone to flatten slightly.

4. Roast at 450 degrees for approximately 80 minutes, rotating occasionally, until a thermometer in the breast shows 150 degrees.

5. Let turkey rest at least 20 minutes before serving.

This method results in a moist, flavorful bird that doesn't take all day to cook.

Wild Turkey Comfort Foods

If you're looking for other ways to prepare your turkey besides roasting it, there are plenty of delicious ways to prepare your turkey.

These ways are all going to assume that the bird was fully skinned, not plucked, so the bird will be skinless.

Turkey Noodle Soup

- 2 wild turkey drumsticks, brined (extra credit: smoke the turkey legs for an hour for extra flavor)
- 2 carrots, peeled and chopped
- 2 ribs of celery, chopped
- 1/2 white onion, chopped
- 2 tbsp. olive oil
- Salt and pepper
- Bay leaf
- 1/2 tsp. dried thyme
- 2 tbsp. chopped parsley
- 1 cube chicken bouillon (optional)
- Egg noodles

Instructions:

1. Fill a pot with water. Add turkey legs and bring to boil. Lower heat to a simmer and then simmer, covered, for 30 minutes.

2. After 30 minutes, take the meat out. Let cool for several minutes and then proceed to shred the meat from the bone. Set meat aside.

3 .Add the bones back to the water and continue simmering for another 45 minutes. If you have any additional turkey parts like the neck or backbone, you can also add these to the water for some additional flavor. Remove bones and other parts from water.

4. While bones are simmering, heat the olive oil in a sauté pan over medium high heat. Add diced veggies and sauté for 4-5 minutes or until veggies are slightly soft and have a light golden color.

5. Add meat, cooked veggies, bay leaf, thyme and parsley to stock pot. Add cube of bouillon for extra flavor if so desired. Let simmer for 10 minutes.

6. Add egg noodles and cook until tender. Taste and add more salt if necessary.

Turkey noodle soup is a delicious way to use up turkey legs.

True, you wouldn't want to just grill up some wild turkey legs and serve them for dinner, but if cooked long enough and mixed in with enough other flavors, you can certainly find a way to use up those turkey legs instead of just feeding them to your dogs!

Wild Turkey Tetrazzini

- 1 package curly egg noodles (or noodle of choice), cooked as directed
- 4 tbsp. butter, divided in half
- 3 cloves of garlic, minced
- 1/2 yellow or white onion, chopped
- 1 cup mushrooms, sliced
- 1/2 tsp. salt
- 1 cup white wine (optional)
- 1/4 cup flour
- 3 cups chicken broth
- 1 cup heavy cream
- 4 oz. cream cheese
- Salt and pepper
- 2-3 cups cubed wild turkey breast (wet brined)
- 1 cup frozen peas
- 2 cups shredded jack cheese, divided in half
- 1 cup panko bread crumbs

Instructions:

1. Preheat oven to 400 degrees.

2. In a large skillet over medium heat, add 2 tablespoons of butter, garlic, mushrooms, and onions. Add salt. Cook just until onions and mushrooms soften.

3. Pour in wine and allow to cook for a few minutes or until liquid has reduced by half.

4. Sprinkle flour over mixture and allow to cook for 1-2 more minutes.

5. Whisk in broth, cream, and cream cheese and allow to simmer for 5 minutes or until thick enough to coat the back of a spoon.

6. Season to taste with salt and pepper.

7. Stir in turkey, frozen peas, cooked noodles, and 1 cup of grated cheese. If skillet isn't big enough, use a large mixing bowl for this step instead.

8. Pour mixture into a greased 9 x 13 inch baking dish.

9. Sprinkle last cup of grated cheese on top of mixture.

10. Melt last 2 tablespoons of butter in microwave.

11. Mix melted butter with the panko bread crumbs and spread evenly over the top of the mixture.

12. Bake 25 minutes or until top is golden and mixture is bubbly.

Baked cheesy goodness, what's not to like?

This is a good way to cook wild turkey breasts. If properly brined, a wild turkey breast tastes similar to chicken (doesn't it all?) but has a somewhat chewier texture that can be off-putting for some.

By chopping it up and making it into a casserole, you can avoid the chewy texture and make a nice, filling, sure-to-please meal instead.

Smoked and Glazed Wild Turkey with Roasted Vegetables

For the brine

- 2 pounds wild turkey breast
- 2 cups water
- 1/4 cup salt
- 2 garlic cloves
- 2 sprigs of fresh thyme
- 1 sprig of fresh rosemary
- Zest from 1/2 an orange

For smoking

- 6 red potatoes, quartered
- 3 large carrots, peeled and cut into sections
- 1 onion, quartered
- 1/2 cup of water
- 4 cloves of garlic
- Fresh thyme sprigs
- Fresh rosemary sprigs
- Zest from 1/2 an orange

For the glaze

- 1/2 cup real maple syrup (can use brown sugar as well)
- 1/4 cup water

Instructions:

1. Brine the turkey. Combine all brine ingredients in a medium saucepan and bring to boil. Stir to dissolve salt and sugar. Let cool completely.

2. Place turkey breasts in a bowl and pour in brine. Cover and refrigerate for 12-24 hours.

3. When ready to smoke, presoak your wood chips for 30 minutes (hickory or maple works well).

4. Preheat smoker to 250 degrees with water bowl filled.

Hunt It, Clean It, Cook It, Eat It | 145

5. Remove turkey from brine and rinse under cold water to remove excess salt.

6. Place vegetables in the bottom of a roasting pan. Lay turkey over vegetables and pour water into bottom of pan. Sprinkle the herbs and orange zest on top of turkey.

7. Smoke for 3 hours or until internal temperature is 165 degrees and vegetables are soft.

8. Glaze—preheat your oven to 400 degrees.

9. Mix together syrup and water until well mixed.

10. Drizzled glaze on top of turkey using a basting brush or back of spoon to evenly coat.

11. Place in oven for 10 minutes to let glaze set. Serve.

Smoking turkey is a great way to impart some additional flavor into your bird. Who doesn't love a great smoked turkey sandwich for lunch?

I know I mentioned above that using aromatics in your brine won't make that much of a difference. I should clarify and say that that's particularly true with plucked birds that still have the skin intact. However, it might make a bit more of a difference when brining straight up turkey breast with no skin on. In this case, I think it's at least worth a try.

Give Turkey a Chance

Hopefully these ideas have inspired you to give turkey another chance. Especially turkey legs.

If you're not partial to turkey, I think the trick is to not make it the star of the show. You don't have to roast it and put it on the table as is. If you smoke it for some additional flavor or mix it in with enough other ingredients so that the turkey isn't the first or only thing you're tasting, you can make yourself a nice meal.

No need to fear the turkey! Embrace it and enjoy yourself a good meal with a fun bird to hunt!

PART THREE
WATER FOWL

Chapter Five
DUCK

HUNT IT

Killing Duck

Waterfowl hunting is a blast (pun intended)! Compared to big game hunting and upland bird hunting, there's a lot of upfront effort and cost involved, but once you're in the field—or water—it's a lot of hurry up and wait. Your aim is to lure the game to you instead of trudging all day in the field trying to sneak up on the game, which is quite different than most other kinds of hunting.

Over the years, hunters realized that, if they can't get close enough to the birds without scaring them off, then they must bring the birds in. But how?

I'm not going to go into the history of duck hunting, but I can tell you how to do it in the modern era. Let's talk about some of the tools of the trade in duck hunting.

When Duck Hunting, Act Like a Scout

You must be prepared for every contingency when you're going out into marshy fields and waterways in the middle of nowhere before daylight.

Fortunately—or unfortunately, depending on how you look at it—waterfowl hunting has one of the most extensive gear checklists. To some, that's part of the allure. They love all the gear needed for a successful hunt.

Below is a list of the most common essentials required for duck hunting. Keep in mind this is just a sampling of the many items you may be required to bring with you on a hunt. The list may vary depending on the season and region where you're hunting. As you become more experienced, this list will keep growing.

Duck Hunting Gear Essentials

- Shells, shells, shells—you can never have too many shot gun shells
- Duck calls
- Flashlight and spare batteries
- Dog whistle (if you're using a hunting dog)
- Duck strap
- Sunglasses
- Binoculars
- Zip ties
- Face mask
- Hand warmers
- Earplugs
- Multiple decoys
- Decoy gloves
- First aid kits—one for humans, and one for canines
- Collapsible ramrod
- Brush clippers
- Electrical tape
- Allen wrenches
- Limb saw
- Spare drain plug for the boat

- Snacks—for both dogs and humans
- License and registration—and a copy of the regulation book
- Knife or multi-tool
- Waterproof bags/boxes
- Seat or stool
- Bug spray and sun screen
- Toilet paper
- GPS/compass

This doesn't even cover the apparel you need.

Dress for Success

When waterfowl hunting, appropriate camouflage that matches the habitat is of utmost importance. Many waterfowl hunters wear a camouflage that mimics the grass blades they hide in. You'll want to know your territory not only so you can match the camo pattern but so you'll know exactly what to wear. If you're teal hunting in Louisiana, you can probably skip the thermal underwear, for instance.

Here's a list of some other apparel essentials you'll need:

- Boots—hiking or rubber depending on terrain
- Camo hat
- Camo jacket and pants
- Gloves
- Insulated pants/overalls
- Waders
- Rain gear
- Socks
- Thermal long underwear
- Face paint or face mask

The last one is essential because there's nothing that will scare birds faster than seeing your face staring up at them!

While you'll hopefully never be trudging around in waist-deep water, it might be helpful to get chest-high waders instead of the hip huggers.

Hip waders won't keep you dry in the boat or the blind after you've been tracking water and mud around all day. Soggy Bottom Boys might be a good band name, but it's not a fun look when you're out in the wind and the elements all morning.

Droppin' Ducks

Unlike upland bird hunting, most hunters will agree that for waterfowl hunting you'll need a 12-gauge shotgun. Duck and goose feathers are surprisingly robust, so you'll need all the power you can get to penetrate their plumage. If you really want to challenge yourself, you can get away with shooting your 20 gauge at a smaller duck species like teal, but for the most part, a 12 gauge is where it's at.

Petite women and junior shooters might consider a 20 gauge if recoil is going to be a big factor, but given that you're more or less stationary when duck hunting, women hunters can get away with a 12 gauge. The heavier weight of a 12 gauge won't be as much of a factor in stationary waterfowl hunting as it is in the more walking-intensive upland bird hunting.

As far as ammo is concerned, waterfowling requires that you use steel shot. This might not seem like a big deal, but for people used to hunting upland game bird with lead shot, you'll need to get accustomed to steel shot.

Here are a few examples of the differences between lead and steel shot:

• Steel is less dense than lead shot and weighs 1/3 less than lead pellets the same size.

• Steel retains less energy and may not kill birds cleanly at the same range.

• Steel shot spreads less and has denser pattern shots resulting in less margin for error.

• Steel shot is better suited to more open chokes like an improved cylinder or modified choke.

As far as shells are concerned, 3 inches is going to be your standard for waterfowl. A 3 inch shell gets you a long enough shell to squeeze enough of the pellets inside to get you decent pattern density with enough oomph for medium to long distance shots.

A 2-3/4 inch 12 gauge shell works if you're going to be blasting ducks at close range. The lighter load might be a good choice for women shooters as well as it helps to reduce recoil.

Three and a half inch shells are also a consideration as it allows for greater shot capacity to make up for the drawbacks of steel shot. As steel shot loads have improved, many people don't find it worth fighting the added recoil or paying the additional price for 3-1/2 inch shells compared to 3 inch ones, however.

There's a lot more that could be discussed when it comes to guns and ammo for waterfowl. Other things you need to take into consideration are barrel length, action, appearance, brand, and cost.

Going into a lengthy discussion about each of these factors is beyond the scope of this book. At the end of the day, gun selection comes down to trial and error and personal preference.

Regardless of which gun you go with, you're going to want to practice shooting before you head out for the season. The more you practice with it, the more you're going to get a feel for what you like and what you need to be a successful waterfowl hunter.

If you shot your gun and find that it's not the one for you, there are places you can go to sell it or trade it for something better suited for you.

Practice Makes Perfect

While in the process of figuring out whether a gun is right for you, there are several things you can do to practice with it to prepare for duck season in the meantime. If you want to be an ace come duck hunting season, doing some of these simple drills in the off-season will help you immensely when it comes time to for the real deal.

Pattern Your Shotgun

One of the best things you can do for yourself is pattern your shotgun. This is especially important if you're new to steel shot. You're looking to do two things when you pattern your shotgun:

Show which combination of choke and load provides the best performance for the type of game you're hunting.

Help visualize how big your game will be at a twenty-five-yard or forty-yard distance, for instance.

Here's what you do:

• Set up a pattern board and cover it with a life-size image of your bird. You can buy ready-made ones or trace your own.

• Move back forty yards and then shoot directly at the image with the shotgun situated in a rest. Since you're just patterning the gun at this point, control for all other mitigating factors.

• Try different chokes and loads to see how each combination performs. Be sure to label each target with the distance, load, choke, and gun used.

• A pattern that has many gaps in it where only one or two pellets strike the bird will need a heavier load or a tighter choke.

• Patterns that have a very dense pattern with little spread might be okay for turkey but indicate too tight of a choke for duck and upland bird.

Once you've patterned your gun, you can move on to other shot improving activities.

Shooting Clays

You don't want the first time you go out waterfowling for the season to be the first time you've shot your gun in a few months. Ideally, you'll have been out at least once or twice a month honing your skills shooting sporting clays or skeet.

If you're going through a sporting clays course, be sure to mimic the way you'll be hunting in the field. Start from a pre-ready position instead of a mounted position, with the stock just below your armpit so you practice raising it to your shoulder as you swing and track the target.

Many times when shooting clays, people will pre-mount their gun to their shoulder, yell "Pull!" and shoot their target. How many times in the field do you have the luxury of pre-mounting your gun as the ducks are flying? Rarely.

Additionally, whether you're shooting clays or just practicing at home, it might also help to shoot at a target from a sitting or low position. This will again help to mimic the real life circumstances in which you'll be shooting ducks and better prepare you come game time.

Ducky Definitions

For someone less familiar with duck hunting, some of the jargon might be a bit confusing at first. Since there are so many species of duck, knowing which ones are which is the first step to becoming a better, more informed hunter. Knowing your ducks will ensure you don't accidentally shoot the wrong one, which can land you a big fine.

Let's take a look at some of common duck terminology:

Puddle duck

A type of shallow water duck that feeds primarily along the surface of the water or by tipping headfirst into the water to graze on aquatic plants, vegetation, and insects.

These ducks are also known as a dabbling duck and are infrequent divers and are usually found in small ponds, rivers and other shallow waterways. They may stay near the shallow, slower edges of larger waterways.

Puddle ducks also forage on land for seeds, grain, nuts, and insects. These are often omnivorous birds and will sample a wide range of foods through their different feeding styles.

Diving duck

Any of numerous ducks, common in coastal bays and river mouths, that typically dive from the water's surface for their food (contrasted with dabbling or puddle ducks).

In general, they take more of the subterranean parts of the plant—winter buds, tubers, and rootstalks, and of the green vegetative parts, than of the seeds. Their diet is supplemented by insects, crustaceans, and mollusks.

Sea duck

Sea ducks are diving ducks that spend most or part of their life in marine or estuarine habitats. Their diet primarily consists of animals like crustaceans, mollusks, and small fish.

> Note: It's important to note that all sea ducks are diving ducks, but not all diving ducks are sea ducks.

List of common puddle (dabbler) ducks

- Green-winged Teal
- Mottled Duck
- Mallard
- Northern Pintail
- Blue-winged Teal
- Cinnamon Teal
- Northern Shoveler
- Gadwall
- American Wigeon
- Wood Duck

List of diving ducks

- Canvasback
- Redhead Duck

• Ring-necked

• Greater Scaup

• Lesser Scaup

• Ruddy Duck

• Masked Duck

List of sea ducks

• American Black Duck

• Eiders

• Scoters

• Harlequin Duck

• Oldsquaw

• Goldeneyes

• Buffleheads

• Mergansers

Now that we're all clear on which ducks are which, let's go hunting!

For simplification purposes, most of the following hunting techniques are going to focus on puddle ducks unless otherwise specified.

Scout It to Count It

As any duck hunter worth his salt will tell you the number one factor to being a successful duck hunter is scouting. As the adage goes, "Scout none, little fun. Scout a lot, hunting's hot!"

There are a couple of different ways to approach scouting. One is the pre-season scouting and the other is the mid-season scouting.

Pre-season Scouting

Pre-season scouting is when you use all of your best resources to scout out several possible locations before duck hunting season even begins. This means:

- Identifying all of the public waterways and wildlife refuges in a given area.

- Looking at topographical maps of the area.

- Contacting some of the county or regional wildlife biologists and officers and asking for recommendations and overlooked opportunities.

- If money permits, doing a flyover of the area in advance.

It's important to identify at least a six spots in advance. Relying on just one or two is putting all of your eggs in one basket. If your spots are already spoken for when you arrive or the ducks just aren't flying, you'll be going home empty-handed.

Once you've identified several spots on the map, it's time to go visit them, making sure to mark exactly where they are on your GPS device.

Terrain looks very different in broad daylight than it does before the crack of dawn. Relying on landmarks will not be a sure way to reach your spot when you're only using a flashlight to get you there.

If you're trying to get off the beaten path to avoid some of the more commonly trafficked public lands, you're more than likely going to have to go through some gnarly terrain. Hitting these spots ahead of time allows you to get an idea of what extra gear you're going to need to bring to get to your spot and exactly how to get there.

You can mark on your maps and GPS exactly where to park the truck, where to launch the boat, and how far down the ducks are feeding. From there you can strategize about where and how to set up your blind for maximum bird action.

Mid-season Scouting

Duck season has started and things were going thanks to your awesome pre-season scouting job. Now after a few weeks of hunting pressure and a change in the weather the birds are starting to thin out.

What now?

This is where your contingency plans come into play.

Why are the birds moving? Has their food dried up? Is there too much pressure from other hunters? Are the waters freezing?

Based on these answers, you can start making educated guesses as to where to head next. You might need to spend some afternoons scouting the next morning's spot. Take a cruise up the river or a drive up the road with your binoculars to see if your hunches play out. If you've identified their roost, see which direction the first few flocks fly.

It's controversial, but there are many experienced hunters who say you should never hunt the roost itself. You do it once and risk blowing the birds out of the area for good.

Some would even argue it's not very "sporting" to hunt in what's essentially the birds' living room. Birds should feel safe in their roost. Oftentimes, the birds are usually at the roost during illegal shooting hours.

But I digress.

Fly-by scouting can also be beneficial. If you put the boat in the water and notice your spot is already spoken for, the water is too low, or there's just no tell-tale signs of birds like feathers in the water, you can always do some on-the-fly scouting.

While you're doing this, you might have the opportunity to jump shoot a few birds while looking for a place to set up your blind.

Resist the temptation to set up in the first spot you see with a few birds. Patience is key, and sometimes you might have to cover ten miles or more to find the perfect spot. It will all be worth it when you flush a hundred mallards and hit your limit of green heads two hours later.

Be Kind, Mind the Blind

Ducks are naturally skeptical creatures. They don't want any sort of human interaction and aren't curious creatures. If they see or sense a human presence, they won't land.

That's why head-to-toe camouflage is mandatory. Your shooting platform needs to be well hidden as well.

The terrain you're hunting will determine what kind of blind you'll need. Some blinds need tall reeds or wooden branches in order to blend in. Wide, featureless expanses require the use of a pit blind, where you sink or dig your blind *below* the horizon so as not to be the only object conspicuously protruding above the horizon.

Duck blinds need not be complicated, however. They just need to keep you camouflaged. Not all duck blinds need to be permanent. They just need to last long enough to get you some birds.

Here are some guidelines when it comes to building blinds and blind etiquette.

Five Truisms About Duck Blinds Every Hunter Should Know

1. Permanent is better but not always possible

It's great to have a go-to spot that you know you'll always be able to bag some birds, but not everyone is so lucky. If you've built, or your area offers, permanent blinds from which to shoot, consider yourself lucky.

2. With portable blinds, you're only limited by your imagination

Some of the best blinds are just some cheap but cheerful creations thrown together last minute out of necessity.

Portable blind ideas can be anything like the following:

- Tying some broom handles together and draping it with camouflage netting.

- Pounding some fence posts in the ground, surrounding it with hog wire, encasing it in oak branches, and laying plywood on the muddy ground for sure footing.

- PVC pipe and grass hula skirts. You're welcome.

3. Duck blinds are like real estate: it's all about location

Ideally, you'll want to situate your blind with the prevailing wind at your back. This way, the birds will make an approach facing you with some nice wing cuppage action, giving you a clear shot.

If nothing else, make sure your blind isn't facing directly into the sun. Make sure you've got plenty of room to swing your gun without hinderance. If you are unable to get the wind directly at your back, make sure all your other ducks are in a row (pun intended) when it comes to setting up your blind.

4. <u>Nobody likes a loud hunter</u>

Apart from your face beaming up at them from below, nothing is more certain to scare the birds off than human voices chatting away. For you it might be more about the fun and camaraderie, but the same can't be said for the hunters several hundred yards away who can hear every word of your conversation along with your hearty guffaws. If they can hear it, the birds can most definitely hear it.

Keep the chit-chat to a minimum and use your "inside voice" if you want to actually bring the birds in.

5. <u>Be punctual</u>

There's nothing more annoying than setting your alarm clock for half-past "not enough coffee in the world" so you can get there early only to have some other guy show up at first shooting light to start spreading decoys.

Way to ruin it for everyone, buddy! Don't be that guy. If you're hunting public land, get your ass out of bed like everyone else or do everyone a favor and stay home.

Bottom line: Good location and camouflage are all it takes for a good duck blind; the rest is icing on the cake. It's also important to know how to be a good duck blind buddy. Keeping some of these tips in mind will go a long way to ensure you don't get skunked or go uninvited to the next hunt.

Don't Be Coy About Decoys

Once you get your blind set up and situated, it's time to lay out your decoy spread. Laying out a decoy spread is more of an art than a science and embodies part of the fun of duck hunting.

The constant trial and error, ever-changing environment, and thrill of finally creating a spread that the birds love is part of what keeps a waterfowl hunter coming back. It becomes like a game of chess with moves and countermoves based on how the birds are reacting.

There are so many decoys and devices nowadays. How does one even know where to get started?

The first rule of duck decoys is that there really are no hard and fast rules about decoys. However, there are some strategies that have proven themselves to be more reliable and productive over the course of time.

If you're just getting started and funds are tight, your best use of money is on your standard mallard decoy. Mallards are the most universal duck and often co-mingle with other species of birds, so they'll almost never look out of place.

As you get more experienced, throw in a few other decoy species as well like pintails for white color, or some coots or black ducks for black color that can be seen from a distance. This is especially helpful in big lakes or flooded fields.

As with many things in nature, size does matter. When thinking about what size of decoy you want to use—standard, magnum, or super magnum—think about what kind of terrain you're going to be hunting.

In close quarters like small potholes and sloughs, the ducks will be working in a close environment, so bigger decoys won't be practical. Not only that, in these cases you often won't be using a boat but rather backpacking in.

Trying to haul magnum size decoys is going to be much more of a slog than hauling your standard decoys, unless you're making several trips to set up a permanent spread.

On the other hand, a larger body of water or flooded field where you'll see the ducks flying in from a distance will require larger decoys to attract their attention. Eighteen magnums will be far more visible than two dozen standards.

Super magnums aren't just reserved for big, open spaces. Flooded timber is also a good place to make use of your larger decoys. The reasoning behind this is that, even though these might be smaller holes, with so much cover from the trees you need to make sure your decoys get noticed and don't get lost in the foliage.

How Many Decoys Should Be in a Spread?

You won't hear too many hunters complaining of scaring away the ducks with too many decoys. In general, more is better than less. That's not to say you can't throw out a dozen dekes and still bring in birds. The circumstances have to be just right,.

Typically for ducks, up to three dozen decoys should do the trick. This gives you enough flexibility to play with various spreads for maximum productivity.

If you're hunting a field where they'll be feeding, you'll need several dozen decoys with a lot of variety. This is when you'll need to enlist some buddies and combine your efforts—and your decoys!—to make the most of terrain.

Better Spread, More Dead

As I mentioned before, decoy spreads are more of an art than a science, but there are a couple of things to keep in mind when setting up your spread.

First and foremost is wind direction. A duck will <u>always</u> land into the wind. When you're setting up your blind, take into account the prevailing wind direction so that it will be at your back or at a quartering angle most of the time.

Make sure to leave adequate room for take off and landing for the ducks, preferably one that's directly in front of your blind.

Here are a few of the most common layouts to use when setting up your spread. Tweaking these as needed for the area where you're hunting is essential.

J-Hook/Fish Hook Spread

One of the most tried and true ways to set up a spread is what's known as the classic J-Hook spread. This is when you set most of your decoys upwind and then run a line of decoys downwind about forty yards away and past your blind, forming a rough J-shape. This leaves a nice landing zone right in front of your blind for you to blast away at.

Horseshoe Spread

Another classic spread is the Horseshoe or U-Shape spread. This is where you concentrate your decoys in a U-shape twenty yards to either side of your boat or blind and forty yards in front of it. Putting a spinner decoy in the landing zone off to one side creates some movement and pulls the birds right in.

Runway Spread

This one works well in shallow water. This is where you set up your boat or blind at the bottom end of the "runway" in the shallows. You'll have birds on either side of your blind in a straight line or at a slight angle with the wide end at the start of the runway and narrowing slightly as it gets closer to your blind. The decoys extend outwards to around sixty yards and almost act as runway lights illuminating the path for the birds to land.

Block and Box

This is particularly useful on streams and sloughs. Most birds will work the main artery of the waterway. You're trying to entice them into a side channel where you'll be in closer proximity. Position most of your decoys upwind, blocking the channel. Then you want to "box" them in by placing a few groups or individuals on the downwind side. You'll want most of these to be on the opposite side of the channel leaving a nice open landing zone for the birds to fly into.

Other Tips and Tricks

A few other things to keep in mind when deploying your decoys:

Motion equals realism

You'll want to incorporate motion into your spreads to make it look more real. The most time-tested of all motion-makers is the jerk string. More recent innovations include wing-spinners, dipper decoys, and water shakers. Use whatever works best for you and your terrain.

Get creative

Place full-body ducks or geese on the land behind or next to your blind if you have a shore blind. Attach some decoys to a log that you float in the water close to shore since ducks often like to rest on logs. This works great where you have a permanent blind set up.

Adapt and adjust

If you notice ducks circling overhead but just not landing, you may need to adjust your decoy spread. There's a good chance that there's something just not quite right about it that's preventing the ducks from landing. Are there not enough decoys? Are there too many decoys (a common late-season problem)? Is there not enough space to land? Have they seen the same spread too many times? These are some of the things you might ask yourself if you notice the birds aren't landing where you want them to or not landing at all.

The art of decoying is part of the allure that keeps duck hunters coming back season after season. It involves an element of strategy akin to knowing which football formation to use against which team. As the game evolves, so must your tactics. This is what ensures the game never gets boring.

To Call or Not To Call, That Is the Question

No doubt anyone who duck hunts long enough will eventually have to learn how to use a duck call. Duck calling can take years of practice to truly master the numerous different sounds one must make to attract birds.

There are numerous sounds that ducks make, like their quiet feeding sound or their more insistent lonely hen sound. Each species has a different trademark sound. Familiarizing yourself with each nuance and variation takes years for some and a lifetime for most.

If there ever was a skill where the "practice makes perfect" adage rang true, it's with duck calling. The time to practice, however, is not when you're on the hunt. If you're still not proficient at duck calling, it's better to leave it up to the veterans when it counts. Nothing will turn a bird off more than an improper or ill-timed duck call.

In fact, I know of at least one lifelong duck hunter and outfitter who advises beginner hunters to leave the duck call at home. His reason: people just don't do it right most of the time, and they lose more birds than they bring in.

If you're a hopeless bird caller, don't despair! It's not the end of the world, and in many circumstances, you should still be able to attract and bag birds regardless.

Duck calling is an effective tool to help lure birds into your spread if done properly. I've compiled a list of ten the best duck-calling tips to help you on your way.

Ten Tips to Better Duck Calling That You'll Thank Me for Later

1. Less is more

You don't have to be constantly duck calling every time you see a flock flying nearby. Not only is that sure to aggravate your blind buddies, but ducks grow wary of calls as the season wears on and might actually actively avoid them instead of being drawn in.

2. Softer is sounder

Loud and aggressive calling might win you points in duck-calling contests but can often be inappropriate in more intimate field settings. Louder calls are okay if you're near big water. Softer is more efficient when you're in flooded timber or other quieter environments. A few muffled quacks might be all it takes to draw them in.

3. Put the decoy for your best call closer to your blind

If you've mastered the lonely hen pining for a drake call, you'll want to put a couple of hens closer to your blind. That way it sounds more natural to any interested drakes flying in.

4. If the ducks are incoming, quit calling

If the ducks have already honed in on your landing zone and are making their approach, your job is done. Back off and quit calling rather than risk mis-quacking and scaring them off.

5. Know when to call

The best time to make use of your loud, aggressive call is when you notice some hesitation from the birds as to whether they're going to turn and come back or keep flying. If they're turning their heads and looking around, hit them with a call. This is when a loud, persistent "comeback" call can be useful. If they're high in the sky and hellbent on getting somewhere, your calls are unlikely to bring them back no matter how loud you're calling.

6. Master the quack

The hen mallard "quack" is the foundation upon which all other calls are based. Hen mallards are the most vocal species, so you'll greatly improve all of your other calls by learning the most common hen mallard quack.

7. Observe and learn

It's one thing to watch a video and get a demonstration of how to use a duck call. It's another thing entirely to go to a pond or lake and actually listen to when, where, and why certain calls are made. A little bit of observation will go a long way toward more realistic calling.

8. Choosing a duck call is important

Just because a friend recommended one call doesn't mean it's going to be the right call for you. Duck calls are personal and individual. Trying them out on your own is the only way you can be assured that you'll get the best duck call for you.

9. Once you find a call you like, buy two

Redundancy is everything in duck hunting: backups are key. Duck calls are no different. Calls get dropped in the mud and water or freeze up, The reed, the small piece inside the call that creates different sounds, can break. Bring a backup with you and leave another one in the truck or at home.

10. Finish your calls

If you initiate a call series, like a feeding or comeback call, see it through to the end even when the duck is responding to it. The duck is expecting a natural progression and any deviation from that is sure to make it think twice about coming in. Once you finish and see them heading your way, back off on the calls and let them cruise on in.

Butterfaces, Duck Calling, and Decoys

Think of duck calling like a hot chick trying to pick up a dude at the bar.

She could be sitting at the bar wearing a smoking hot red dress that hits in all the right places. Some nights, she doesn't have to do anything but sit there and wait for the guys to come over and chat her up. Other nights, though, the dudes might be distracted by a game of pool or the juke box in the corner.

A soft cough or sexy laugh at just the right time is all she needs to get a guy's attention. Once he looks her way and likes what he sees, he'll come in for a closer look.

If she gets his attention and he *doesn't* like what he sees—a butterface, for instance, where everything looks good but for one crucial part: the face—he's going to keep on playing his game of pool instead.

That's like duck hunting. Your calling is going to get the ducks' attention but the decoys and the spread are really what's going to pull them in. Your duck call can either be the sexy laugh that's like music to the ears or the loud belch that will make a guy do a hard left and detour to the bathroom instead of heading toward the "lady" at the barstool.

The call and the spread work in tandem. They both have to be just right in order to pull the birds. A good call with a bad spread will kill your odds of bagging a bird as easily as a bad call with a great spread.

If the woman in the red dress looks good enough, a dude will just beeline right for her anyway without her even trying.

Same thing with a decoy spread. It's helpful, but not mandatory, for you to use a call to attract a bird to your spread. If your spread is off, no amount of calling in the world will get it to come in and commit.

The Three Unsavory Types of Duck Hunters You Never Want to Be

Before we wrap up, we need to have a little chat about some of the most unsavory kinds of hunters you'll encounter while waterfowling. You'll learn to spot them a mile away and hopefully prevent yourself from being that guy and ruining it for everyone.

Skybuster

This is someone who shoots at anything and everything that flies overhead. This is a big no-no in duck hunting and a common error for the less experienced and more excitable waterfowl hunters.

This tends to happen in a couple of circumstances. Either your spread isn't bringing the birds in close enough but you try and shoot at them anyway, you're jumpy and trigger happy, or you have bad vision and really can't tell how far away the birds actually are so you shoot at them just in case.

If you have to tilt your head way back and point your gun almost straight up in the air, you're probably a Skybuster.

One of the most common mistakes in duck hunting is shooting too soon. Take your time and let the decoy spread and calling bring the birds in close enough so you can take a reasonable shot.

Ideally, anywhere within the forty-yard range is an acceptable range to shoot at a bird. Once you get outside of that range, you risk wounding the bird and not killing it, especially with less forceful steel shot. If the bird is too far away, you risk dropping it in an area where you or your dog will never be able to retrieve it, essentially wasting the bird.

Skybusting also scares the birds off. If you're taking shots at birds that you realistically have no chance at hitting, they're going to get spooked and just leave the area. They won't just fly three puddles over, they're going to fly three counties over where you'll most likely never have a chance of shooting at them again.

Googans

Googans aren't exclusive to duck hunting, but they're a pervasive species nonetheless.

A googan is someone who thinks they know how to hunt (or fish or surf or boat, etc.) but really has no idea. They just picked the sport up recently and know just enough to be able to do it unassisted but not enough to really understand proper etiquette.

They might have gone out on a guided hunt once or twice and think they know everything there is to know and that they can do it on their own now. Instead of doing their own scouting, they show up at someone else's spot that they've visited before. They might not have mastered their duck call yet and are loudly blowing away on it, scaring ducks away for miles. You can usually spot these guys because they have the latest, most expensive gear but no idea how to use it.

In general, these are the hunters who ruin it for everyone else with their lack of etiquette or real knowledge of how to hunt.

Muggers

Muggers are often a type of googan. These are the guys who hear you blasting away at birds from a half mile away and decide to motor on up to within a couple hundred yards of you and try to set up a spread.

They're the ones who probably didn't do any scouting themselves and are just trying to go wherever they hear a hot tip or have seen other hunters staking out.

After they've gone out of their way to close in on your spot and see the birds starting to decoy into your spread, they'll actively call them away from your spread and into theirs.

Don't. Just don't. So not cool.

Outfitters who take hunters out for a living lose clients over this practice when some googan or mugger is out hogging all the spots that the outfitters painstakingly spent hours and days scouting before the season even began.

Not only have they ruined that day's hunt, but they've potentially ruined a part of someone's livelihood by preventing them from providing a top-notch experience for their clients who likely won't come back if their paid hunt is ruined by the constant presence of know-nothing hangers-on.

In short, don't be one of these guys. Go with a guide until you're sure you won't be polluting the waterways with your poor etiquette and lack of expertise and ruin it for everyone.

A Special Kind of Crazy

If you're still keen to get started duck hunting despite all the factors that would turn many people away—the crazy early hours, the huge expense to get started, the often cold and blustery or wet and muddy conditions—then you might be a special sort of crazy.

Yes, duck hunters are a special kind of crazy, but that's because duck hunting is a special kind of sport. It's different than your typical big game hunt, and it has the power to draw you in like no other kind of hunting.

In my experience, that's the best kind of company to be in. Happy shooting!

CLEAN IT

From Taxidermy to Table: Unconventional but Efficient Ways to Clean and Care for Your Birds After the Hunt

After you've shot your limit of ducks, it's time to clean them up so you can try out some of the many tasty recipes!

Fortunately, cleaning ducks is a fairly simple matter not unlike most other forms of bird cleaning. There are a couple of unique ways you can clean a duck that you wouldn't use with other birds.

Let's go over some of the most common techniques used to clean a duck.

Field Care

First things first: we need to discuss what you do with your ducks after they've been shot. Quality field care is always essential and the first step to ensuring a tasty meal later down the line.

Field care for ducks is pretty straightforward.

The first thing you need to take into consideration is the temperature. If it's warmer than sixty degrees out when you hunt, you need to get the birds cooled down as quickly as possible. This requires separating the birds—not piling them on top of each other. You can do this by laying them out in a cool, shaded area.

If you're not in an area where you can lay the ducks out, put them on a duck strap. Don't just stuff them in a bird bag and leave them there. Once on a strap, you can hang them in a shady spot until you're ready to transport them.

From there, you can place the ducks in a plastic bag and throw them in a cooler filled with ice. It's not recommended to throw the ducks directly on top of the ice, as the water can aid in bacteria growth. If you do put the birds directly on ice, make sure the drain of the cooler is open so that the water drains as it melts. You don't want those birds sitting in a pool of blood water for the rest of the day!

Any bird that has been gut shot should be gutted immediately. All other birds can be left intact and stored until reaching their final destination where you can proceed with skinning or plucking them.

It's also important to know both state and federal regulations about waterfowl identification. Be sure to clip and keep a wing, a leg, head, or thigh for identification purposes should you come into contact with any wildlife regulators if required.

How to Make Your Taxidermist Love You

I can't talk about field care without mentioning how you would care for a bird that qualifies for your Wall of Fame.

There may come a time in your hunting career where you shoot a bird that's just too pretty to eat. You'll want to treat this bird a little bit differently than you do the ones you're planning on eating.

Late season mature birds are the best for mounting. Not only are their colors typically more vibrant but they usually won't have pin feathers, which fall out during mounting.

If you shot your trophy and find it still alive, the best way to dispatch it is by sticking a small pocket knife in through the mouth and up through the brain. Just be careful not to stick the knife through the head. Whatever you do, DO NOT wring the bird's neck. That's a no-no if you want it to be a pretty mount on your wall.

Carry the bird by the feet and not by the neck. You want to be as delicate with the bird as possible and handle it how you would be handling the mount itself. You also want to avoid using a game strap to carry it. Treat it with kid gloves.

When you get home, gently rinse any mud or blood off the bird with cold water. Pat it dry and place it in a plastic bag with the neck folded up against the body. Roll the bag so the air is forced out of the bag, and seal it. Place this bag inside of another bag, and seal it.

You can then freeze it for up to a year until you're ready to take it to a taxidermist. Don't take a bird that has been chilled but not frozen for more than forty-eight hours.

Do not gut or skin the bird yourself. Also, do not expect to get any meat back from your taxidermist. They cannot guarantee the safety of the meat and most will not risk the liability of returning meat that someone could potentially get sick from.

While you're in the field, you don't set the bird down on cold metal, like a boat bench. It can get stuck or frozen there, and you might pull feathers out when you have to rip it off.

You'll be guaranteed to have a trophy of the One That Didn't Get Away to show off for generations to come!

Never Ask a Hen Her Age

Before we go into how to clean and/or pluck the birds, we need to discuss a point of contention amongst hunters—whether or not to age your game bird.

Many hunters swear by aging their ducks because, just like most other meat, it becomes more tender and flavorful after aging due to the enzymes breaking down some of the protein in the meat.

The thought of aging one's waterfowl makes many other hunters' stomachs churn, however.

If you're the curious sort and want to try it out, here's what you should know about aging your duck:

- Leave ducks whole as you age them. Most agree there's no need to gut them unless they were gut shot to begin with, in which case you're assuredly better off just skinning and breasting them right away.

- Hang the birds from either the neck or the feet, both are okay to do.

- Ducks can be aged anywhere from 2-14 days. Longer than 14 days is not recommended as there is no significant improvement in texture or flavor after 14 days.

- Birds should be hung at a temperature from 34-50 degrees. Consensus seems to say that 45-50 degrees is ideal. Aging at temperatures above 60 degrees is not recommended as the spread of bacteria multiplies significantly at those temperatures whereas there is little to no bacteria development at temperatures below 50.

- Dry pluck, do not wet pluck, the bird after aging (we'll talk more about this in further sections). The skin is looser after aging and will tear more easily if you wet pluck after aging.

Aging a bird doesn't just apply to ducks. It's quite common to age pheasant, chukar, and other game birds as well.

174 | Haley Heathman

If it's not something you've ever tried before, do a side-by-side experiment with duck that's been aged versus a non-aged duck and see if you notice any difference in taste or texture between the two.

Many people who age their ducks say that this negates the need to brine them. This is a matter of personal preference. Do a taste-test and find out.

There's no wrong answer to this. It comes down to what you want, so don't be afraid to experiment a little to find out the best way to prep your birds before cooking.

When in Doubt, Breast it Out

By far the most common and easiest way to clean your duck is to breast it out. This means peeling the skin back and removing just the two breast halves that lay beneath with a sharp knife. Breasting out a duck is the easiest way to clean a duck in the field.

There are a couple of different ways to do this. One way is to simply grab the duck by the skin and peel it back along the breast like you're opening a shirt or a jacket. Pull the skin back far enough to expose the whole breast. From there, run a sharp knife along either side of the breast bone and cut out the breast.

Some hunters make this easier by plucking a few of the down feathers from the breast of the duck. They then make a small incision with their knife on the skin, which makes it slightly easier to peel the skin back from the breast area and you just proceed as described above.

The "It's a Snap" Method for Cleaning Ducks

Remember in the upland bird section where I detailed the "it's a snap" method for cleaning your pheasant?

There's an equivalent method for cleaning your duck, although not exactly the same.

If you recall, with pheasant cleaning you bend over, stand on the wings, grab the bird by the legs and gently "snap" up, which pulls all the guts out while leaving the breast intact on the ground.

We do sort of the reverse with that breasting method when cleaning a duck:

1. Pluck a few feathers and pull the skin back from the bird just enough to expose the breast.

2. Lay the duck on the ground breast-side up.

3. Put one of your feet on the head and the other on the tail of the duck.

4. Put one finger under its breast at the top near the wishbone and another finger under the base of the breast near its tail end.

5. "Snap" up with your fingers gently pulling the breast away from the rest of body.

6. Once it's pulled away from the body, you'll be left with the breast with the wings attached in your hand and the rest of the duck on the ground.

This is an especially useful technique in the field as it doesn't even require use of a knife. Pulling out the breast while keeping the wings attached to the bone fulfills the identification requirement in many states.

If you want to keep the heart or gizzards, you can easily remove them and put them in a small plastic bag for storage. You can also remove any other parts of the duck you wish to keep like the legs, thighs, head, neck, or the pope's nose if there's any delicious fat down there that would make tasty cooking oil later.

While breasting out your bird is the simplest and easiest way to clean it, many hunters consider it extremely wasteful and disrespectful to only breast out your bird and leave the rest behind.

For various reasons it may be necessary to only use the breast. If you never take the time to pluck it whole, use the carcass for duck broth, render the fat for cooking oil or make sausage from the off cuts of the bird at least some of the time, then you're doing that bird a disservice.

Take the time to educate yourself about some of the other things you can do with your duck besides just breasting it out. I'll teach you some things in the next chapter but there's so much more beyond even that.

There's a reason why duck is a staple protein in so many cuisines—it's such a versatile and delicious bird when prepared correctly by using all the parts the duck has to offer!

Pluck, Pluck, Goose

I think birds are almost always better when they're whole. If you ask me, chicken skin should be its own food group as far. It's no different with most other kind of fowl.

Although time consuming, plucking your ducks can be the first step in what's destined to become a delicious meal down the road.

Plucking and cooking your ducks whole is pretty much only recommended for puddle ducks. It's generally not recommended for your diving ducks because of their high protein diet. Most of the fishy flavor will be retained in the skin and fat of the bird and will not be tasty if you roast it up whole.

As I'll discuss more in depth in the next section, diving ducks are better off used for stews, gumbos, sausages, and other foods where the duck itself isn't going to be the star of the show but one of many components and flavors mixed together.

Now that we've gotten that out of the way, let's talk plucking ducks!

Dry Plucking

Dry plucking is just what you would imagine plucking a bird to be. This is where you just sit the bird on your lap and pluck away. It's easiest if the bird has already been cooled down significantly as the feathers will give way much easier.

Dry plucking is time consuming but it results in a beautiful bird most of the time and produces more consistent results than wet plucking. Once you've done it enough, you can dry pluck a bird in about ten minutes. Beginners should expect to take about thirty minutes to pluck a duck.

Here's the step-by-step process of dry plucking duck:

1. Start with a whole bird. Do not gut the bird. Do not clip the wings or legs until the end.

2. Pluck the wings first. These feathers are the most hardy and are the most difficult to pluck. Pluck the feathers closest to the body and just beyond the first joint.

3. Once the wings have been plucked, move on to the breast. Holding the body down with one hand, use your thumb and forefinger of the other hand to pluck up and away from the body, as if you were pulling a tuft of grass from the ground. Don't grab too many feathers at a time. This is down feather and should be pretty easy to pull out.

4. Exercise more caution around where the bird was shot. The skin will be much more delicate in this area and more liable to tear, so go slowly while you pluck this area. Anchor the skin around the shot while you pluck around it.

5. Work your way toward the tail feathers and then start to pluck those out. Only pluck one or two feathers at a time. These will pull straight out.

6. Move on to the backbone. Anchor the bird by the feet with one hand and pluck with the other. You can do this side fairly quickly.

7. Grab the bird by the wing to expose the "armpit" of the bird. Gently pluck these feathers out. The skin is thin here so go slowly so as not to tear it.

8. Finally, you can work on the legs. The feathers here are small and hard to grab but fortunately there aren't a lot of feathers.

9. This should give you a general rough pluck of the bird. From here you can do a little bit more detail work in some of the areas you might have missed before. If you miss a few, that's okay. After it's plucked you will then gut the bird. When you rinse it under cold water you can gently rub off any remaining feathers you may have missed.

10. At this stage, you can start cutting off the extremities. Using some heavy duty kitchen shears, you can clip the wing at the joint closest to the body. The reason this wasn't done at the beginning is because the skin will recede once it's

clipped and it will be much harder to pluck those feathers near that joint.

11. Using your kitchen shears, you can then snip off the neck. Take it off maybe an inch above the body. There will be a little neck nub remaining which you can snip off by pulling the skin back a bit towards the tail end and snipping it off with your shears.

12. Lastly, remove the feet. Cut them just where the feet start to meet the skin. It should be all tendon here and no bone, so it shouldn't be that difficult to clip.

Voila! Your duck is now ready to be gutted, rinsed, and turned into a beautiful and exquisite meal.

Wet Plucking

Wet plucking is a somewhat faster albeit slightly uglier way to pluck your ducks.

The process of wet plucking your ducks involves a big vat of steaming, but not boiling, water. Usually around 140-150 degrees is a good scalding temperature. The purpose behind wet plucking is that the scalding of the bird will make the feathers easier to pull out.

1. While you're waiting on your water to reach temperature, pre-pluck some of your birds. Pull out some of the large wing and tail feathers so the water will more easily penetrate the rest of the bird.

2. Once the water reaches temperature, grab the bird by the neck or the feet and dunk the bird for about 30 seconds. Swirl it around a little bit so the water penetrates the feathers. Some people even add a few drops of Dawn dish liquid to the vat because the soap helps to dissolve the water-proof oils that coat the duck's feathers, which helps the water to penetrate the feathers faster.

3. You only want to dunk the birds just long enough that the feathers pull out quickly. Any longer and you risk boiling your bird.

4. Pull the bird out of the vat and let it drip dry for a few seconds. From there, pluck the bird immediately while it's still warm using the same technique outlined above.

The process should go a little bit quicker with the feathers having been loosened up a bit due to the scalding.

The Wax Method for Plucking Your Ducks

The last method is similar to the wet plucking method but involves using paraffin wax to aid with removing the feathers.

You're going to need two vats or basins of water. In the first vat, melt the paraffin wax over hot, but not boiling, water. Fill the second basin with ice water.

For this method, you're going to need to use a lot of wax, so stock up in advance! Use about a block of wax for each large duck and a half a block of wax for each smaller sized duck.

Make sure to prepare your ducks in advance. This requires removing any broken wings (less you'll have to pluck later) as well as pre-plucking some of the larger, stiffer feathers in the wings and tail area. The wax method really only works on the down feathers of the bird.

Give just a brief pluck to some of the back and breast feathers, too—just enough to get it patchy.

1. Pre-pluck about fifty percent of the feathers off the bird. Be sure not to pluck down to the skin as you don't want the hot wax to scald the skin.

2. The last step of prepping your bird for the wax is to clip off the wing at the first joint since you won't be eating it. You don't want it using up some of your expensive wax!

3. Now you're ready to apply the wax to your duck! Hold the duck by the neck and dunk it into the vat of hot wax. Most of the wax will be floating toward the top of the water, so swirl it around a bit at the top for about ten seconds until just coated.

4. As soon as the duck is coated in wax, dunk it into the bucket of cold water for about thirty seconds to set the wax. Lay the bird to the side for a few moments to dry off.

5. Once the birds are dry, you're ready to take off the wax. The wax should be hardened and have formed a nice crust around the bird.

6. Crack the wax at the neck and at the wing to start breaking apart the crust. Once you get these cracks in the wax, start pulling chunks of waxy duck feathers away from the neck and wings.

7. After that, work toward the backbone. Bend and/or squeeze the duck just enough to get some fissures in the wax or until you hear it pull apart from the skin underneath, then start tearing away the wax in chunks from the back.

8. Finally, you'll work your way to the breast. Work gently around the breast area as the skin can be a little more delicate here. Keep removing chunks of waxy feathers off until you reveal all of the gorgeous, pimply skin underneath.

And there you have it! A quick and less time-intensive way to pluck your duck. It can be more costly this way due to the abundance of paraffin wax you'll have to use, but the pay-off will be less time spent plucking your ducks and a much more clean, presentable whole duck ready for roasting in the end.

Now Go Eat

We've gone over proper field care for your birds as well as the most common ways to clean them. Now it's time to learn what you can do with once they're clean and ready for cooking.

COOK IT

Delicious Duck Recipes Sure to Delight

Ducks are interesting. If you ask me, they might be one of the most unique species of wild game out there because there are so many species of duck and they all have something different to offer, including their flavor.

Many words have been written about which ducks are best for eating. If prepared correctly, pretty much any duck is delicious, even the lowly sea duck. Some are just tastier than others, or at least take less effort to make them ready for the dinner table.

The top five most edible species of duck are:

- Wood duck

- Teal (in particular green winged teal)

- Mallard

- Pintail

- Widgeon

These are just the top five most agreed upon species of duck. They're not ranked in any particular order because it's just a matter of personal preference. Unsurprisingly, they're the puddle ducks that live land-based for a good chunk of the year and have more corn, rice, and soy in their diet than diving ducks and sea ducks.

Beauty and the Bufflehead

In the case of sea ducks and diving ducks, beauty really is in the eye of the beholder. These birds *can be* delicious, but you're limited in the parts you can use and the way you prepare them.

For all but the most dedicated wild game enthusiast, you're not going to want to pluck and roast them in the oven and eat them as is.

Instead, breast them out (no whole birds here), brine them for at least a few days, and then turn them into some sort of stew or gumbo, not make them the protein-based star of your meal. You can also turn these into some sort of sausage, laden with tasty pork fat and other flavors and seasonings.

Under no circumstances should you take the fat and crisp it up in a fry pan. Instead, rid sea ducks and diving ducks of every single ounce of fat it has, including any surrounding the offal.

The fat is what's going to harbor the flavor of what the duck has been eating. Fat that's laden with the flavor of crustaceans and algae is stomach-churning stuff sure to induce your gag reflex.

The one exception to this *might* be with bluebills, aka scaups. In the San Francisco Bay area, they tend to dine mostly on clams and clams are much milder than fish and other shellfish.

This exception holds true only if you see a nice white layer of fat surrounding the duck instead of the usual orange layer of fat typical of a diet primarily of seafood. White fat almost always indicates a mild, neutral tasting duck.

If you see the typical orange layer of fat, abort your mission immediately. It's going to taste horrible, and you should revert back to cooking it like you would any other sea duck or diving duck.

To Brine or Not to Brine?

We talked about brining in the turkey chapter and how it helps to reduce gaminess and softens up the tough parts of the bird. What about ducks? Do ducks need to be brined as well?

Well, that depends. If we're talking diving or sea ducks and you're not going to turn them into sausage or jerky, I'd say yes.

As for the puddle ducks, especially those mentioned earlier in the chapter, it depends on personal preference and who's going to be eating the ducks. You don't have to brine them to make them edible like you do sea and diving ducks. Some people enjoy the taste of a fresh mallard or teal.

Personally, I'm not in love with the flavor of duck. I put myself in the "must brine" category. Not only do I brine the ducks, I do so way more aggressively than I do wild turkey.

For turkey, put it in your saline bath for twelve to twenty-four hours and you've got a moist, delicious bird. Duck, being a dark-meat bird, requires more frequent and longer brining to truly cleanse the bird of the livery flavor common of dark-meat game.

With duck breasts, put them in a saline bath like you would the turkey. When it comes to duck, the water should be changed out every twelve hours for three to five days until the water is free of sediment.

You'll notice that, when brining your duck, the water will turn slightly pink. This is from the saline forcing the blood out of the meat. The blood stored in the meat is what gives it that livery flavor. If you want to get rid of that flavor altogether, brine the duck until you notice no more pink water, which indicates all the blood has left the meat.

Now you should have a tender, mild-flavored piece of game meat that you can serve proudly.

If you've got some sea ducks or diving ducks that you want to cook, you absolutely want to be brine those babies for three to five days and make sure you get every last bit of blood and sediment out of the meat. You do not want that muddy, fishy flavor or smell permeating your meat as it will not be tasty. This will help with the texture of the diving duck, which is known to be tougher and stringier than most puddle ducks.

For puddle ducks, it's a matter of preference. Duck season just opened, and I gave a nice, rare sear to a beautiful, fresh piece of mallard we'd just shot the day before. While the texture was perfect—tender and easy to chew—I couldn't get past the slight livery taste.

I brine my duck no matter what. You *can* get away with not brining your puddle ducks for as long as your diving ducks. Even just one go in the saline bath will make a great improvement to the flavor and make it just that much more mild.

I like to go through at least two or three rounds of brining, dumping the water, and replenishing with a fresh brining solution with my ducks, but if you really enjoy the flavor of fresh duck meat, you can get away with less on most puddle ducks.

Duck Fat... Mmm!

Somewhere along the way in the last fifty years or so, our society decided that fat was bad. Fat, which we had been living off of since the dawn of time, was suddenly Public Enemy Number One. Instead of butter, we were told to eat margarine. Instead of bacon fat, vegetable shortening. Instead of olive oil, vegetable oil.

All of those "instead ofs" are chemical imitations of real, natural products that have long been part of the human diet.

Whether out of fear of fat or just in the interest of saving time, most hunters will discard all the tasty fat and just save the meat. On diving and sea ducks, this is perfectly acceptable. With puddle ducks, think about saving and rendering that liquid gold.

In general, wild game is known to be leaner than commercially sold meat. This is true of ducks, but not always. Depending on what part of the season it is and what the duck has been eating, you might come across a perfectly plump duck full of rich, white fat from the rice fields. When you do come across such ducks, think of it like hitting the wild game jackpot.

In the culinary world, duck fat is a delicacy. Many restaurants will go out of their way in their menu descriptions to indicate when an item has been fried in duck fat. Potatoes and French fries are some of the most common things to be cooked in duck fat.

Duck fat has a high smoke point, meaning you can cook foods at an extremely high heat without burning the oil or altering the flavor. This makes duck fat a good choice for making crispy potatoes, searing meats, or just roasting your vegetables for added richness and flavor.

Unlike most other cooking oils, duck fat is reusable, so instead of scraping the remainder into the trashcan, spoon it back into your mason jar and use it again later.

Let's take a deeper look at how to render your duck fat.

Duck, Duck, Fat!

To render duck fat, take the fat from the fattiest parts of the duck's body: the butt, around the base of the neck, and from around the gizzard. Use at least one pound of duck fat to render down, which will make around one cup of rendered duck fat.

Here are step by step instructions to rendering duck fat into liquid cooking gold:

1. Cut the fat from the duck's body.

2. Cut the fat into small pieces, around 1 inch pieces.

3. Place fat into skillet. Fill skillet up with water so that the water goes at least halfway up the fat.

4. Simmer on medium heat. The mixture will be cloudy and milky looking.

5. Once the water is mostly boiled away, around the halfway point, turn heat to low. As the water fully evaporates, the liquid will become clear. It will take between 45-90 minutes for all of the water to evaporate out.

6. When you have a clear, golden liquid, get ready to strain. Set up a glass measuring cup with a mesh strainer over the top. Put a paper towel inside of the mesh strainer to catch the impurities. Pour the fat in batches through the strainer and into the measuring cup. One pound of fat should render to around 1 cup of fat.

7. Pour rendered and strained fat into mason jars. The fat will last from nine months to a year in the refrigerator or can freeze indefinitely.

Now you've got some liquid cooking gold to use on your finest recipes!

Sweet, Sweet Duck

It's recipe time! I'll specify whether a particular recipe is good for all ducks (puddle, diving, or sea ducks) or if it's only good for certain kinds of ducks.

For our purposes, please review the criteria presented above regarding brining/not brining when deciding whether to use brined/unbrined duck in each recipe.

Duck Gumbo

- 2-3 cups wild duck meat, sliced
- 1/2 cup canola oil, divided
- 1/2 cup all-purpose flour
- 1 pound smoked sausage, sliced
- 2 cups chopped onion
- 1 1/2 cups chopped green pepper
- 1 1/2 cups diced celery
- 2 tbsp. fresh parsley, chopped
- 1 tbsp. minced garlic
- 1 15 oz. can diced tomatoes
- 2 bay leaves
- 2 tbsp. Worcestershire sauce
- 1 tsp. pepper
- 1 tsp. salt
- 1 tsp. dried thyme
- 1/4 tsp. cayenne pepper
- 1 quart of chicken or duck stock
- 1 quart of water
- Cooked white rice

Instructions:

1. In a Dutch oven or large stock pot, heat half the oil over medium heat. Add duck pieces 1 cup at a time and brown. Remove from oil and set aside.

2. Add additional 1/4 cup of oil to pot or enough to equal 1/2 cup of oil. Add flour to the oil. You want equal parts flour and oil. Cook and stir over medium heat until brown, around 10-12 minutes.

3. Add the sausage, onion, green pepper, celery, parsley, and garlic to the pot with flour mixture (also known as roux). Cook for 10 minutes, stirring occasionally.

4. Stir in the rest of the ingredients except for the rice. Add the duck back in as well and bring to a boil. Reduce heat. Cover and simmer for 60–70 minutes or until the duck meat is tender.

5. Serve with rice.

If you want to go all out, make a stock with the carcass of the ducks boiled with some onions, carrots, and celery. You can also smoke the duck in advance to give it even more depth of flavor.

If you prefer to keep it simple, this recipe will still make a delicious gumbo recipe that will be suitable for all types of duck, but in particular diving ducks or sea ducks.

Gumbo is a great way to cook diving and sea ducks. You can use all of the meat on the duck so long as you make sure there's no fat lurking about.

There are enough other flavors in the gumbo to mix in with the duck so that it's not the star of the show. Even if there is a slightly fishy taste or smell to it, it's not out of place in a gumbo, which often has crawfish or shrimp pieces in it. Slow cooking the duck for an hour or more will ensure it's more tender than tough.

This should be a staple duck recipe for any hunter as it can be a catch-all recipe for all varieties of duck.

Duck Stir Fry

- 4 skinless duck breasts
- 1/2 onion, sliced lengthwise
- 1/2 red pepper, sliced lengthwise
- 1 bunch of green onions, sliced into inch long pieces
- 3 tbsp. peanut or canola oil
- 1 tbsp. sesame seeds
- 1 tbsp. corn starch

Marinade:

- 1/4 cup soy sauce
- 2 tbsp. sesame oil

- 1 tbsp. rice wine vinegar
- 1 tbsp. fresh grated ginger
- 1 tbsp. minced garlic
- 1 tbsp. honey

Instructions:

1. Slice duck into thin strips around 1/4" to 1/2" thick.

2. Mix all marinade ingredients together in a small bowl. Add duck to marinade in the bowl or sealable bag. Place in fridge and marinate for 60 minutes.

3. While duck is marinating, prepare all other ingredients. Slice veggies, prepare wok (or large skillet), and have all other ingredients ready to go.

4. Take duck out of fridge.

5. Heat 1 tbsp. of oil over high heat in your wok. Let oil heat up for 1-2 minutes until it shimmers and just begins to smoke. Add onions, peppers, and green onions to wok and stir fry 1-2 minutes. Remove from heat and set in bowl.

6. Add the remaining 2 tbsp. of oil to pan and allow to get hot. Add sliced duck to the wok, reserving marinade. Stir fry duck until brown on all sides.

7. Quickly mix corn starch into reserved marinade and pour on duck. Return stir fried veggies to the wok along with sesame seeds and let cook for 1-2 more minutes or until the sauce turns glossy.

8. Remove from heat and serve with rice.

This is another recipe you can use with your "off" ducks like diving ducks or sea ducks. The strong Asian flavors will neutralize any fishy or otherwise gamey flavor the ducks might have.

That's why it's important to use skinless ducks in this recipe. If you're using diving ducks or sea ducks, that skin is going to be no good and will infuse your food with a strong fishy smell and taste.

If you have ducks that have a nice layer of skin on them, you're better off cooking them in such a manner that shows off that skin, like in this next recipe.

Pan-seared Duck Breast with Cherry Pan Sauce

- 2 skin-on duck breasts
- Salt and pepper
- 1 tbsp. butter or bacon fat

For the sauce:

- 2 cloves of garlic, minced
- 1 tbsp. shallot, minced
- 1/4 cup of chicken or duck stock
- 1/4 cup fruity red wine like merlot or pinot noir (if no red wine, use 1/4 cup of stock for a total of 1/2 cup)
- 2 tbsp. cherry jelly (can also use red currant, cranberry, or blackberry jelly)
- 1 tbsp. butter
- Salt and pepper to taste

Instructions:

1. Bring duck to room temperature on a counter top for 30-60 minutes before cooking. Season both sides with salt and pepper.

2. In a stainless steel or cast iron pan (you want the brown bits in the bottom to make the sauce), add butter over medium high heat. Allow pan and butter to heat up, then add duck breasts skin side down to pan. Cook 3-4 minutes per side for a larger duck, 2-3 minutes per side for a smaller duck. This should be a nice rare to medium-rare temperature. It is not recommended to serve duck above a medium-rare temperature.

3. Remove duck breasts from heat and set aside to rest while you make pan sauce.

4. Remove all but 1 tbsp. of any fat left in the pan, just enough to coat the bottom.

5. Add garlic and shallot to pan over medium heat and sauté for 1 minute or just until soft.

6. Deglaze the pan with the red wine. Allow to cook down for 1 minute, then add the 1/4 cup of stock. Scrape pan with a wooden spoon making sure to get all the brown bits from the bottom of the pan which add a lot of flavor.

7. Stir in the jelly and cook until jelly is fully incorporated into the sauce and sauce is thick enough to coat the back of a spoon.

8. Remove from heat and stir in pat of butter. Serve over sliced duck breast.

This is a great, simple way to cook your skin-on duck breast from some of your better eating puddle ducks like widgeon, teal, or pintail.

The most time-consuming part of this whole process will be plucking the ducks so you can have that nice, tasty bit of skin to sear off in the first place. But once you get down to cooking it, the whole recipe shouldn't take more than 10-15 minutes to cook.

Duck Ragu with Pasta

• 4 bone-in duck legs and thighs, preferably skin on
• 1 tbsp. olive oil or duck fat
• Salt and pepper
• 2 celery stalks, diced
• 2 garlic cloves, smashed and peeled
• 1 small onion, diced
• 1 carrot, chopped
• 1 tbsp. fresh sage, chopped
• 1 bay leaf
• 1 cup dry red wine
• 1 can crushed tomatoes (28 oz.)

- 1/2 to 1 cup chicken broth
- 1 pound pappardelle or wide noodle pasta of choice, cooked al dente

Instructions:

1. Heat oil over medium-high heat in a heavy duty pot or Dutch oven.

2. Season both sides of the duck legs and place them skin side down in the pot. Sear until nice and brown, around 7 minutes. Take your time with this part. You want the legs to have nice sear. Turn legs over and sear other side 2-3 minutes more.

3. Transfer duck legs to a deep platter and pour off all but 1 tbsp. of oil.

4. Reduce heat to medium-low. Put all veggies and herbs in the pot. Cook, stirring frequently, until veggies are softened, around 5-6 minutes.

5. Pour in the wine and increase heat to medium-high. Simmer for 1 minute and then reduce heat to medium. Stir in tomatoes and 1/2 cup of broth.

6. Return duck to pot and reduce heat to medium-low or low to maintain a gentle simmer. Cover pot and simmer until meat is falling off the bone 1 1/2 - 2 hours, possibly longer for larger birds like mallards. Don't rush this step.

7. Remove duck from pot and set aside to cool. Skim excess fat off the top. If sauce seems thin, continue boiling until it thickens up.

8. Discard the duck skin and shred the meat from the bone. Add the shredded meat to the sauce along with more broth if sauce seems too thick. Let the sauce simmer gently 10-15 minutes. Season to taste with salt and pepper.

9. Serve with your choice of pasta.

This is a great choice for your Sunday supper. Like most Italian sauces, it's better if it's prepared a day or two in advance so the flavors have time to mingle. It may look like there are a lot of steps, but they're all easy steps that require little technical skill apart from patience.

Many hunters throw out the duck legs—it's just easier to breast out the duck and throw away the rest. If you're the type who hates seeing things go to waste, slow cooking or braising those duck legs and wings is a good way to make use of every part.

Unlike the breast, which you want to cook hot and quick, the legs are much tougher and need to be cooked low and slow like any tough cut of meat to tenderize it.

You can use this method to do your duck legs in a number of different ways:

- Braised duck leg nachos

- Braised duck leg carnitas/quesadillas/enchiladas

- Pulled duck barbecue sliders

- Duck stroganoff

Duck for Days

Duck is truly one of the most unique wild games out there. There are so many varieties of wild duck which means there are numerous ways to kill it along with several ways to clean them based on how you want to eat it.

In terms of cooking, duck is a staple food in so many different types of cuisine—from Asian to French to Italian—that you can turn your wild duck into almost any kind of dish you could imagine. It's really limited only by your imagination.

Once you get the basics of cooking duck down like how to clean it, when to brine it, which ones are best to eat, and how to cook the various parts of the duck, your culinary world will open up more than you could have ever imagined!

Hopefully now you'll be inspired to dream big with your duck. Much of the fear around cooking duck should be alleviated now that you know which ones to cook and how.

With most duck seasons being around 100 days with limits of around seven per day, you now have the skills to make it a new staple of your wild game repertoire!

Chapter Six
GOOSE

HUNT IT

Everything You Need to Know to Be a Goose Hunting Hero

If you've read through the duck chapter that preceded this one, then you'll already have a lot of the information needed to be a solid waterfowl hunter. But despite the similarities in duck and goose hunting, there are a fair enough number of differences that merit a full separate section to goose hunting. There is a lot of crossover but there are a few important differences you must be aware of when hunting goose that I'll go over in this chapter.

While hunting them is similar, cooking goose is a whole other animal (pun intended)! Let's get on with what makes goose hunting different from duck hunting and discuss all your options when it comes to what type of gun and ammo you'll need.

Guns 'N Ammo

For many of the same reasons as I discussed in the duck section, you'll more than likely want a 12-gauge shotgun for taking down geese. Anything less and it might not wield the power you need to make a kill shot, especially at passing geese that you'll be shooting at longer distances.

However, you might find a 10 gauge more helpful with larger species of geese. A 10 gauge is often better for bigger loads than what you would use with a 12 gauge. While there is a place for a 10 gauge, the 12 gauge is still more commonly used.

A discussion of specific makes of shotgun and which one is best for goose hunting is beyond the scope of this book. If you really are stuck on this question, seek out some experts at local sporting good shops.

The bigger question then becomes what kind of ammo you need.

There's a little bit more nuance to this question as we must consider a few different circumstances.

- Is it early season or late season?

- Are you shooting decoying geese or passing geese?

- Do you plan on shooting only geese, or are you going after ducks as well?

These considerations will inform you as to which # shot you'll need to make clean, ethical kills.

Technically speaking, the range of shot you could use when hunting geese can vary from #4s all the way up to T shot. But just because you can doesn't mean you should.

Can you kill a goose with #4s or #3s? Sure, if you're shooting it from extremely close range and it's early season when they're not as fat. I kill flies with table salt when shooting them at point blank range with my salt gun. You *could* kill a goose at near point-blank range with #4 shot, but you most likely won't get the opportunity to shoot that close.

If you're shooting at anything greater than thirty yards, those little #3s and #4s are barely going to penetrate the feathers nonetheless make a clean kill.

Moving Up, Let's Consider #2 Shot

Twos are a good choice if you're going to be both duck and goose hunting and shooting over decoys. It packs enough of a punch that it will make a clean kill for close- to medium- range geese. Plus, it's not so heavy that if you do take a shot at some ducks it won't obliterate them.

While #2s are doable—and an acceptable choice if you're multi-tasking with your hunting—for exclusive goose hunting you're going to want to use anything in the #1 to BBB range.

This is when you really need to consider what kind of hunting you're doing. If it's early season when the geese are typically lighter in plumage and not as fat yet, #1s are a good choice, especially if you're going to be shooting more at decoying geese than passing geese.

If it's later in the season when the geese have put on more feather and fat, you're going to want to use BB or BBB shot. In certain places at specific times of the year, it's going to be very difficult to get geese to decoy. Either they're hellbent on getting further south or they've grown very wary of a big decoy spread because they've seen so many of them. You'll be taking a longer shot—around sixty yards or more—and are going to need bigger pellets to penetrate at that long range.

If BBB is good for long-range passing shots, then T shot should be even better then, right? Not necessarily.

T shot, while bigger and heavier than BBB, often patterns too thin to make an effective shot. While some people swear by Ts because they're so deadly, many hunters believe that T shot is only for skybusters who want to shoot at anything and hope for a lucky shot.

If you do decide to go with a T shot, you're better off using it with a 10 gauge than a 12-gauge gun. It's proven very effective against some of the larger geese like Canada's, but less necessary on some of your smaller geese like Snows.

Gray Goose Got You Feeling Loose

And the light goose… and the dark goose…they'll all get you feeling loose once they're lying on top of one another in a nice pile near your blind!

Similar to how ducks have a classification system—puddle ducks, diving ducks, and sea ducks—geese are also grouped into distinct families: dark geese, light geese, and gray geese.

Dark Geese

Dark geese are going to be comprised mainly of Canada geese. These are the most commonly known type of goose with the characteristic black head with the white cheek patch that runs from the chin to just behind the cheeks.

The other main species of dark geese is the Cackling goose. The Cackler is almost indistinguishable from the Canada goose except that it is significantly smaller in size. There are also several sub-species of cacklers such as the Aleutian, Taverner's, and Richardson's.

Light Geese

Light geese encompass primarily two species of geese: the small Ross's goose and their well-known cousins, the Snow goose.

As you might suspect, light geese are lighter in color, almost entirely white with just some dark tips along the wings, although snow geese do have some white and blue color variations.

The lesser snow goose has seen an explosion in population growth over the past couple of decades, particularly along the West coast. Measures have been enacted to allow longer and more favorable hunting conditions for this species in an attempt to control their numbers.

Gray Goose

The most common—and most-prized—among any goose species is the Greater White-Fronted goose, aka Specklebelly, aka Speck. These are almost universally considered the best tasting of all the goose species and are highly sought out by hunters. Hunters often affectionately refer to them as the "ribeyes of the skies!"

Specks are primarily gray with a gray head but get their name from the black and white markings on the chests of the adults.

Specks nest pretty far north near the Arctic Circle in Central Canada and migrate south early.

Other less common types of gray geese include the Brant—which are primarily coastal birds that you'll find on both the Pacific and Atlantic coasts—and Emperor geese, which spend the majority of their life up in Alaska.

Field of Dreams

Here's where we'll get into one of the most important differences between duck hunting and goose hunting.

You do the majority of duck hunting by boat or at least require a boat to get somewhere you can set up a blind on land.

With goose hunting, you'll be hunting on land and in fields just as much as you do on the water. In some regions, particularly in Canada and other northern states when they just start to migrate, all you'll hunt is land with very little hunting done from a boat at all. While geese eat some aquatic plants, they much prefer grain and grasses when they can get it.

Geese are creatures of habit. A standard day in the life of a goose goes something as follows:

They will roost on a large body of water overnight. They're generally not as early-rising as ducks and tend to push off a touch later than ducks to head off to eat. The feeding grounds are often an agricultural field nearby where they'll spend a couple hours before heading back to smaller water to loaf. They might make one more trip to the feeding ground later in the afternoon before going back to their roost for the evening.

There are a few exceptions to this schedule, of course, one being the weather. Geese will often stay in the field feeding for most or all of the day if it's raining or snowing.

Another exception is hunting pressure. If they're feeling highly pressured, they'll vary their pattern or just leave the area altogether for greener pastures, so to speak. This is why many hunters say it's a big no-no to hunt the roost as you'll just push the birds out of the area.

One final exception to this pattern has to do with moon phases. I'll go into more depth about moon phases later on but for now just know that if you're not paying attention to moon phases when hunting geese, you're probably wasting your time several days out of the month with fruitless hunting endeavors.

Finding the X Spot

If you want to be successful in goose hunting, you're going to have to be familiar with the X Spot for optimal goose hunting opportunities.

The X spot is exactly where the birds want to be. As the old saying goes, "X marks the spot" is where you'll find your buried treasure. In this case, the treasure is flocks of birds all descending on your exact location wave after wave.

There's a lot of talk about "hunting the X" when it comes to goose hunting, but how do you find it?

Again, this is where your scouting is going to be of utmost importance. It's impossible to overestimate the value of thorough scouting before any waterfowl hunt.

If you've identified the roost where the geese have spent the night, grab your binoculars and find some higher ground, if possible, several hundred yards away.

As the sun comes up, watch as the first few flocks fly away toward the feeding ground and note which direction they're going using a GPS or compass. Drive that direction, stopping along the way to get out and glass from a safe distance until you see the landing zone where dozens, if not hundreds, of geese are happily feeding, usually in a nearby grain field. You've found the X spot.

The good news is that, as I mentioned before, geese are creatures of habit and will likely return to the same spot day after day as long as there is still food available. All you have to do is secure permission to hunt the field where they're feeding and do the hard work of trailering all your decoys out to the field early the next morning.

Almost Doesn't Count

You might be feeling pretty excited that you've managed to find the X spot and are anxious to head out and start setting up your decoy spread.

You get to the field where you saw them the day before, get your spread set up and your layout blinds ready to go. Your call and flags are ready, now you just wait for the birds to fly in.

There they are! Your heart starts pounding in excitement as they fly your direction. Here they come! Then you watch in dread as they fly overhead and land seventy-five yards behind you. Oh no!

What happened?

You were close, but you weren't on the X. You were on the wrong corner of the right field.

It's happened to every waterfowler at one time or another where they just barely missed the spot where the birds want to be. Sure, you can manage to call some over your way and get a fair few birds. But nowhere near as many if you had managed to set up on the X. It may not sound like a lot, but even fifty to seventy-five yards can make a difference between a good day hunting and a great day hunting.

There is something to be said about *not* being on the X. Some hunters deliberately don't set up on the X itself, either as a matter of personal preference, they didn't get permission to hunt the land, or it's impossible to access.

The thing to do in this situation is to hunt the traffic lanes. If you know where the roost is and where the X is, find a place where you can set up directly between the two spots. You'll still be able to call in a good number of passing birds as they're on their way to the X.

In these instances, you might not be able to get them to decoy all the way, but you might be able to get them close enough for a passing shot. If you can't hunt the X, hunting the traffic lanes may be the next best thing.

The Laws of Attraction: Three Winning Ways to Woo Geese

In New Age-y speak, the Law of Attraction is the ability to attract into your life whatever you are focusing on, often by using the power of the mind to translate whatever is in our thoughts and manifest them into reality.

Whatever you say.

We can still use this principle, at the heart of which lies the simple maxim that "like attracts like," to become better goose hunters.

In our case, the laws of attraction have more to do with our calling, flagging, and decoying than it does laying in a blind in the freezing cold willing the geese to come closer with the power of our minds and positive thoughts.

Perhaps even more so than in duck hunting, your ability to get the attention of and attract geese is fundamental to success.

The "Match the Hatch" Technique

Like in duck hunting, camouflage is of the utmost importance. Geese are very sharp-eyed and will be able to spot something that's not quite right from way off.

The name of the game is to "match the hatch." This phrase is used in fly-fishing when determining which fly to use, but it is equally true when goose hunting.

It means that your camo and your blind need to blend in as much as possible to the surrounding area. If you're hunting in the snow up in Canada, you'll want to be wearing all white, not woody brown camo.

With goose hunting, camouflaging your blinds can be a bit trickier than with duck hunting. Since you'll be hunting in big open fields, large, vertical sit-in blinds are going to look quite a bit out of place to any passing birds.

If you can make use of any natural formations from which to hide behind, such as hay stacks, rock piles, or fencerows, those are often the safest bet even if they might be slightly off the X.

Barring that, your other best option is a field blind that you can lay in and spring up and shoot from once the birds get close. You'll want to blend in as much as possible so make sure to drape as much of it in natural cover as possible using any resources available to you.

Matching the hatch also refers to your decoy spread as well. Take note and be aware of how the birds are grouped when they're flying. If you don't see more than thirty birds flying together, you shouldn't put more than thirty birds in a field together.

You'll also want to match your decoy spread to the time of season. In early season hunting, for instance, Canada geese are still in their extended family groups. When setting out your decoys, keep them in groups of around six to eight full body decoys to reflect that situation, again "matching the hatch."

You might have noticed by now that you'll be using way more decoys with goose hunting than you do with duck hunting. Whereas you can get away with a few dozen duck decoys, you'll often need hundreds of goose decoys. This is especially true when you're hunting the running traffic, such as when you're setting up in between the roost and the X. You'll need a particularly large decoy spread to attract the geese from where they were initially headed.

While a large decoy spread is the first step, it's not the only step when trying to attract those geese your way.

The "Call it to Haul it" Technique

Your camo is on point and your decoys are spread out in an irresistible formation with plenty of runway space right in front of your layout blinds for them to land where you'll be ready to shoot.

In duck hunting, there are times when your decoy spread alone will be enough to attract the birds to your elegant trap. When field hunting geese, that is rarely the case, and your ability to attract passing geese's attention with loud and well-timed calls is of crucial importance.

If you want to be a successful goose hunter, you're going to have to practice your calling. This will probably take years and years of practice, much like playing an instrument.

In order to help you with that, here are some helpful tips to help you master the art of the goose call.

Five Practical Pointers to Help You Master the Art of Goose Calling

1. Master the long-range call and the cluck first

The long-range call is crucial to getting passing birds' attention and getting them to look your way. Once they turn your direction, transition to a cluck call. Let the cluck act as a beacon to draw them in until they're within range. These two calls will go a long way to getting you started with luring in geese.

2. Read your birds

Calling at anything and everything that passes by isn't going to increase your chances of getting a shot. You must learn to recognize the difference between birds that are hellbent on getting somewhere you're not, birds that aren't going to look your way no matter how loud your call is, and birds who are looking for a spot to land and to whom your calling will be like sweet music to their ears.

3. Don't overcall

More often than not, overcalling will end up scaring birds off more than pulling them in. One of the exceptions to this is when hunting public land, and there are numerous other groups all competing to lure the birds in. Loud calling can sometimes result in the birds decoying on your spot versus someone else's. Especially during late season hunting, the birds have been honked, clucked, and called at for months on end and are extremely wary. When in doubt, less is more.

4. Short-reed calls are becoming the go-to call for goose calling

If you're in the market for a goose call, you should look at short-reed calls first. If you do most of your goose hunting over water, look into flute calls. They are more muffled, which is better because sound travels faster over water. The loud short-reed call can often be too loud for birds over water but is the perfect choice for birds in field.

5. Practice, practice, practice

Practice in the off-season to ready your lungs and keep your calls sharp. Practice the calls you haven't quite mastered. Practice in your car on the way to work. Watch YouTube videos. Just keep practicing.

Once you've called your birds and gotten their attention, it's time to bring them on home.

The "Flag it to Bag it" Technique

Flagging geese can be an extremely effective way of getting their attention and bringing them in. Combined with proper calling, this can be a deadly duo that will get you your limits time after time.

What is flagging? Is this when you stake a country's flag in the ground and hope they're wooed by national pride?

Hardly! Flagging involves making motion with a black T-shaped silhouette loosely resembling a flapping goose. This is attached to a pole which you raise, flap, and lower to the ground to imitate geese landing or stretching near your decoy spread.

Here are some tips to make the most of your flagging so you can bag those birds:

204 | Haley Heathman

Five Flagging Tips That Will Make Your Spread Impossible for Geese to Ignore

1. Bigger is better

Calling usually requires restraint, with flagging you want to go big or go home. When the birds are still far away, make big motions with your flag. With their sharp eyesight, they can spot you up to a mile away. Using big motions will catch their attention from a distance.

2. Keep flagging

Even once the birds have turned your direction, keep flagging, but as they get closer you want your motions to be smaller and more subtle. Just as the calls will pivot from long-range hails to quieter feeding clucks, flagging should pivot from big motion to more subtle flurries as they approach. Keep flagging even after shooting into the flock. Sometimes it will bring them back around for a second pass.

3. Flagging can be more effective than calling

Especially in late season when they've grown wary of excessive goose calls, flagging might be a better way to attract geese than lots of vocalizations.

4. Vary the pole lengths

Some hunters use poles six or even ten feet in length. This creates a bit of distance between the flag and the blind so the bird isn't focusing its attention directly on you. The longer poles also help create bigger motions for long-distance birds. Short poles around four feet in length are good for when trying to imitate a stretching bird and are easier to work as the birds get close.

5. Flag on the turn

If they're circling the perimeter of your spread, as they're circling to turn away, hit them with the flag. You want them to catch the motion out of their peripheral vision. Flagging as they're staring at you straight on might look less realistic than just a bit of motion in their side vision as they're turning off and entice them to come back.

These three techniques—the "Match the Hatch," "Call It to Haul It," and "Flag It to Bag It"—are going to be your triple threat when it comes to slaying those geese. If you get these three things down, you'll be a master goose hunter in no time!

Full Moons Aren't Just for Werewolves

I touched on this briefly in a previous section and now it's time to go into more detail about how moon phases affect goose hunting. If you're not paying attention to your moon phases while you're waterfowl hunting, you're probably spending a few wasted days a month without much success.

What do full moons have to do with waterfowl hunting?

It alters the birds' feeding and roosting behavior. This goes for both duck and goose but is especially true of geese.

Geese will often reverse their feeding and roosting behavior during a full moon. Instead of roosting at night and feeding during the day, geese will feed at night under the full moon and then spend most of the next day loafing.

While a full moon is only one day per lunar cycle, it's full enough on the day or two before and after that the birds will usually exhibit this behavior for at least a few days around the full moon.

For hunters, this means if you're up early in the morning the day after the full moon and are anxiously awaiting the birds to fly to the field you're in to feed, you'll probably be waiting quite a long time. The geese have already been feeding all night long and will spend most of the morning loafing on water at their roost until they push off again later in the afternoon to feed again for a good part of the night.

Not only do their feeding behaviors change, but many geese will migrate during a full moon as well. In addition to their feeding patterns having changed, a lot of birds will have pushed out of the area so there are fewer to shoot in general.

206 | Haley Heathman

That can be good news a few days after the full moon when a new crop of migrating birds descends upon your area. Hunting can be quite hit and miss right around the period of the full moon, but it can be red hot just after it.

To compensate for these new patterns, more savvy hunters will refrain from morning hunts during the full moon phase and settle for afternoon hunts when the birds push off again. These afternoon hunts can often be very fruitful and create many banner days of waterfowl hunting.

Weather Trumps All

Now that you've added lunar cycles to your calendar and list of waterfowl behaviors to be aware of when hunting, I'll throw in a quick caveat even to this: *weather trumps moon.*

If it's cloudy or stormy during a full moon phase, then the birds won't change their feeding patterns after all. The cloud cover will negate any benefit of feeding under the moonlight, and the geese will happily stay in their roost all night and carry on their normal feeding pattern.

Lunar cycles and weather forecasts are two more of the many moving pieces of the puzzle that avid hunters need to put together if they want to be successful waterfowlers.

Go Forth and Get Ye Some Goose!

Armed with all this knowledge and fresh with new techniques to use, you'll be ready to hit the fields and hit your limit in no time! If you're serious about hunting geese, you'll need to know some tricks of the trade as how to clean those suckers once the bodies start to pile up. Those Canadas are big and can be quite a pain to clean, but I'll teach you some tried and true ways to be a goose cleaning expert in no time!

CLEAN IT

Spruce Your Goose Like a Pro

Geese are a lot of hard work. This is true all around, from hunting it to cleaning it. They are far more cunning than ducks and require much more work to get them to decoy, hence why some spreads require hundreds, if not thousands of decoys to get a flock to come your way for a closer look. This also becomes a deterrent for many people when it comes to hunting them. It can be a pain, to say the least.

The amount of work involved in setting up the spread, waking up at the ridiculous hour you have to get up, and then, if you have a successful hunt, figuring out what to do with that huge pile of goose bodies once you've taken them down.

The final nail in the coffin is that many people just don't really like the taste of wild goose. The breast can be extremely tough. To cook them whole can be very greasy, not to mention time consuming to pluck. Due to the amount of blood in the meat, they can taste excessively livery, or gamey.

For some hunters, goose hunting can be a lot of work for little reward if you consider your reward a tasty meal as a result of your efforts.

I'm here to get you to reconsider all of that. In this chapter, we'll focus on the best ways to skin or pluck your goose (and when it's best to do each) and ready it for a delicious meal.

Skin It or Pluck It?

Like ducks and most other game birds, skinning or breasting out your meat is by far the easiest way to deal with your game after you've shot it. There are times when you should consider taking the time to pluck your goose whole.

Here are some guidelines as to help you determine when to skin and when to pluck your goose:

- Specks are always a good candidate for plucking. They are universally recognized as the best tasting of all the geese, if not of all waterfowl. You'd be doing that bird a huge disservice if you just breasted it out and threw away the rest.

• You can pluck Canada geese as well, especially if they've been wingshot, leaving the breast meat pristine. Some of the sub-species are small and manageable and less cumbersome than Greater Canadas, for instance.

• Snow geese and other light ducks should be skinned. Even though they are smaller than Canadas, they are typically less fatty and can have blueish skin that's in no way appealing. However, if you take a peak and notice pink skin on the breast instead blue, you can get away with plucking that bird as that bird has a nice layer of fat on it.

Now that you've determined whether to skin or pluck, let's talk about how to do it.

Breast Is Best

There's not much that's different about breasting out a goose than there is to any other type of wild bird. It takes slightly more work to expose that breast area than on other birds, however.

To start with, you'll want to pluck about a two-inch by six-inch section of feathers straddling either side of the breast bone and continuing the length of the breast.

From there, make a small slit in the sternum just large enough to expose the breast. You can then tear the skin back off the breast exposing the meat. It's certainly doable to just tear the skin back, but if you're adept with a knife, you can use it to cut the skin away from the meat down to the rib cage.

Take your sharp knife and make an incision along the side of the breast plate from top to bottom. Continue on along down the ribcage until you've freed all the meat from the bones. Place the breast in a bowl of water until ready for future use.

But What About the Rest?

There are plenty of hunters out there who consider it extremely wasteful to only breast out a bird and not use any other bits of it. Many hunters will rationalize this by saying that there's very little additional meat outside of the breast to use on a goose. They'll argue that the leg has very little meat and is usually not very tasty.

This is true and not true all at the same time.

The legs of a goose aren't necessarily delicious to just fry up on their own and eat, but they can be used for other things like stocks if there's not enough meat worth saving. The same thing goes for other parts of the bird like the internal organs, the wings, and the carcass. If you know what you're doing and want to take the time to do it, goose legs and wings can actually be delicious on their own.

While it's true that the breast provides ninety percent of the usable meat on the goose, that doesn't mean that the rest of it can't still be utilized.

Like Duck, Like Goose

Fortunately, cleaning a goose is similar, if not identical, to how you would clean your duck. The same techniques I already discussed in my duck chapter are all equally pertinent to goose.

Since they are much larger, it is generally not recommended to dry pluck your goose. Dry plucking takes considerably more time than wet plucking, and if you have more than one goose to clean it will take you forever. Wet plucking, where you scald the bird in hot water first to loosen the feathers, is a better method which will enable you to pluck your bird more quickly, if not more messily, than dry plucking.

Especially with larger geese, the wax method I discussed in the duck chapter is going to be your best bet.

With geese, you'll probably need to use two blocks of paraffin wax to get enough waxy coating on the bird. Doing it this way will save you a considerable amount of time compared to wet or dry plucking the bird.

Plucking the bird will give you many more options with what to do with it when it comes time to cook it. You can still just breast out the bird, but this time with the skin on, and use the carcass for stock. You can use the internal organs for other delicious dishes. Like with duck, goose fat is a delicacy and extremely tasty to cook with.

Get Loose With Your Goose

There's really not much more to say about how to clean a goose that's different from how you would clean a duck. Cooking goose, though, can be a bit tricky and require more manipulation than simply throwing the breast on the grill as soon as you've cleaned it. We'll go over some of the techniques you'll need to make your goose sensational and worth the effort to shoot and clean in the next section!

COOK IT

The Whole Enchilada: There's More to Goose Than Just the Breast

Oh, the lowly goose. Probably one of the most misunderstood and underrated fowl and game species out there when it comes to cooking it.

I'll raise my hand and stand guilty as charged on this count as well. Goose was, and to an extent, still is, intimidating to me.

I've not eaten much goose in my life, not even domestic goose. While cooking a domestic goose is a relatively simple affair, trying to tame the wild goose and turn it into an elegant dish—tender in texture and mild in flavor—is a bit more challenging than with many other wild game species.

What is life without a little challenge, right? That's part of the joy of hunting—the challenge. It's part of life's eternal battle of man versus beast, man conquering nature, man taking what nature has to offer and turning it to his benefit.

We're not going to let some overgrown bird beat us, are we (although geese can be some mean suckers when they want to be)? No!

Fear not the wild goose! We're going to learn how to conquer goose in the kitchen as well as in the field. Let us not feel guilty anymore about killing a goose but not eating it or not using the full extent of its bounty.

Read on to find out some tips, tricks, and recipes that will get you and your guests saying, "Ooh, la, la!" the next time you're fixing to serve up some wild goose.

Brine It, Soak It, Age It, Eat It!

Even more so than wild duck, wild goose will probably benefit from any combination of the above to mellow out the gamey flavor imparted from the excess amount of blood that resides in the meat. I've talked about each of these techniques in various forms in other game species and you can try them in any combination for goose as well.

Many hunters recommend aging your geese for at least a couple of days before plucking or butchering them. As explained in the duck chapter, aging just requires that they be hung up in a cool, dry area below fifty degrees fully intact. This allows some of the blood to drain from the body and allows the enzymes to help break down the meat to make it more tender.

From there, you'd then begin your plucking or bird cleaning process. If you're just going to be breasting out the bird, I'd recommend brining them or soaking them in some sort of solution for at least a couple of days. This will help rid the meat of excess blood, which is what causes the livery, gamey flavor that many people find distasteful.

To brine the breast, you'll just need to submerse the meat in a salt-water solution. I'd use about 1/8 to a 1/4 cup of salt in the solution. If you're going to be brining for multiple days, you don't want your meat to get overly salty, so go with smaller doses. You can increase the amount of salt in your brine if you're going to be brining for one or two days.

If you're uncertain about brining, soak the meat in milk. This works for any kind of meat, wild or domestic, goose, duck, beef, or chicken. The enzymes in the milk can help break down the proteins in the meat which helps to tenderize it. Most people who do this usually only soak their meat for one night. Milk tends to be more expensive than water or salt water, so soaking for multiple days and changing out the milk can get expensive.

There are some people who merely soak their goose breast in plain water to get the blood out of the meat. People also think that it will probably make it moister, but I remain skeptical on this count.

When doing an experiment with turkey breast that was brined in a salt-water solution versus just soaked in water, the turkey that was just soaked in water ended up losing more moisture during the cooking process than one that was brined. The salt ions that permeated the meat cells help retain moisture throughout the cooking process resulting in a moister turkey than one that was soaked in water. I can't imagine the science of this somehow miraculously changing from one type of meat to another.

For you science-y types out there, you can always do a little experiment yourself and see which method produces the best results: brining, soaking in water, or soaking in milk. If you do, I'd love to hear your results!

Cure It? I Didn't Even Know It Was Sick!

If you haven't had any sort of wild goose charcuterie, you're missing out! Turning your goose breast into a prosciutto you'd serve on a gourmet cheese platter will turn any wild game skeptic into a believer.

I know a lot of people who can't stand the livery taste of a baked wild goose breast but who go gaga over thin slices of cured goose breast on a cracker with some smoked gouda.

While the thought of curing your meat sounds complicated, it really isn't. It just requires some time and patience. Here's all you'll need to do a basic goose breast prosciutto:

Goose Breast Prosciutto

- 1 full goose breast, skin on
- 3/4 cup kosher or pickling salt
- 1/4 cup sugar
- 2 tbsp. garlic powder
- 1 tbsp. ground fennel seed
- 1 tbsp. white pepper
- 1/2 tsp. ground clove
- 1/2 tsp. ground nutmeg

Instructions:

1. When you breast out the bird, make sure to leave as much skin and fat on the bird as possible, including the fat "tails" on both the tail and neck ends of the bird.

2. Mix all the spices together in a large bowl. Coat the goose breasts in the mixture thoroughly. Rub the mixture into every bit of the meat. Place any remaining mixture into a non-reactive container just large enough to hold the goose breast. Place the breast on top and cover.

3. Let the breast cure in the refrigerator for 1-3 days. The bigger the bird, the more time it will need to cure. Flip the bird over at least once a day so that both sides get even contact with the extra cure.

4. When the breast is done curing, rinse and dry the breast off thoroughly. The breasts must be fully dry after rinsing. Lay the breast skin side down on a rack for at least an hour or two to aid in full air drying.

5. Now that the breast has been "cured," it's time to hang it. Try and find a humid place (60-85% humidity), that is between 40-60 degrees to hang your goose prosciutto. Poke a hole in one of the skin "tails" left on during the breasting process and hang from a string or S-hook. Make sure the meat isn't touching anything else. Let hang for 2-3 weeks. Longer hanging will result in more complex and deeper flavors.

Easy peasy lemon squeezy!

The only thing that becomes slightly problematic is finding a place with the right temperature and humidity. Some people opt to allow the meat to dry out in a refrigerator. This works well to control the temperature, but the humidity is often fairly low. This can cause the meat to dry out more quickly, so a shorter drying period is needed.

In higher humidity settings, keep an eye out for mold growth. White and green mold is normal and can be countered by spritzing and wiping the meat off with some red or white vinegar. If you see black mold forming on your meat, unfortunately it's gone bad and you risk serious health consequences if you try to rescue it.

One way to increase humidity is by hanging the meat over a container of water. You can also spritz it every day with a bit of water if it's drying out too quickly.

After you've practiced the recipe a few times, play around with the spices you use to cure the meat with to create different flavors.

You don't even need to be a doctor to "cure" a goose breast! All you need is a bit of time and some patience.

Thank You for Smoking

I love smoking meat. Any kind of meat. All of it. Almost all meats can be improved through the process of smoking.

This is especially true of wild goose. Something magical occurs in that hot box of flavored air particles. Instead of masking the gamey/livery flavor that wild goose can be known for, the smokiness actually complements the wild game flavor and enhances rather than overpowers it. The result is a delicious piece of meat that is complex and robust in flavor without ruining the integrity of the meat itself.

Smoking is a great way to cook a goose that has merely been breasted out with no skin. Prior to smoking, the breast will benefit from some brining in advance. Marinate the breast for at least a few hours. This will impart some additional flavor that will go a long way to complement, but not totally mask or overpower, the natural flavor of the meat.

If the breast has already been brined for several days, cut down the amount of soy sauce used in the recipe below to just a couple of tablespoons so as not to make the meat too salty. Otherwise, you can cut down on your brine time by a day or so since you'll also be marinating this in soy sauce.

Between the marinade, the brine, the smoke, and the natural flavor of the meat, these components all combine to create a well-balanced, but complex interplay of flavors and aromas.

Smoked Citrus Goose Breast

- 1/2 cup orange juice
- 1/3 cup olive oil
- 1/4 cup dijon mustard
- 1/3 cup maple syrup
- 1/4 cup soy sauce
- 1/4 cup honey
- 1 tbsp. onion powder
- 1 tsp. garlic powder
- 2 large or 4 small-medium goose breast halves
- 1 cup hickory or mesquite wood chips, soaked
- 8 slices of bacon* (optional, see note below)

Instructions:

1. Whisk together all marinade ingredients in a bowl. Place goose breasts in dish, pour marinade over, turn to coat once or twice, then cover and place in refrigerator. Marinate 3-6 hours.

2. Preheat a smoker to medium heat, around 300 degrees. Once ready, put the wood chips in the tray.

3. Smoke goose breast until rare to medium rare, internal temperature of 135 degrees (temperature will continue to rise as meat rests). Start checking internal temperature after around 30 minutes and every 10-15 minutes thereafter. It shouldn't take more than 60 minutes to get to temperature.

4. Let meat rest, then slice crosswise and enjoy with sides of your choosing.

Note: If you did not age, brine, or soak your goose breast in anything beforehand, wrap your goose breasts in bacon while smoking them. The bacon drippings will prevent the breast from getting too dried out during cooking and help keep it moist.

You can wrap the goose breasts in bacon even if you did brine it if you want to because bacon makes everything better, right?

It's *crucially important* that you keep an eye on your internal temperature of the goose breast while smoking it. This is going to be a far better indication of doneness than cooking time, especially because wild goose breast will vary considerably in size.

As with all other wild game meat, you do not want to overcook your goose breast. This will make the gaminess more pronounced as well as make it super dry and tough. Goose is already inclined to being a tough cut of meat. Overcooking it can darn well make it inedible, both in terms of texture and flavor.

Done right, however, and this will become one of your staple goose recipes for years to come.

Know How to Use Those Legs

One of the most tragic mistakes of cooking wild goose is not using the whole bird. Many hunters justify this by saying, well there's not much meat on the rest of the bird anyway. This is true, most of the meat is found in the breast, but what meat there is on the legs is quite tasty and delicious if you know how to prepare it.

The other reason hunters don't bother with the legs is—I hate to say it— just plain laziness.

Plucking a goose is time consuming. I get it. No one says you have to pluck every bird you shoot, but you should be aiming to pluck around 25-50% of them. If you can't be bothered to do the birds you killed that courtesy, then maybe it's time to cut back on the number of birds you kill. After all, that's probably the number one criticism of hunting by non-hunters: it's barbaric.

Every hunter I know of counters this by saying they eat all the game they shoot. Fair enough. But does it really count if a hunter regularly only takes the choice cuts of their game and discards half or more of the rest?

I'm not saying you should feel obligated to go so far as to make down pillows from all the feathers you plucked from your birds (although that's not uncommon). If you routinely only ever breast out your goose without ever making use of any of the rest of the parts, it's time to start rethinking that.

This recipe will help. This gives you a fabulous way to make use of those goose legs that will get you a delicious dish that you didn't even know you were missing!

Easy Roast Goose Legs

- 4 to 8 goose legs, skin on
- Salt
- Duck fat, butter, or lard

Instructions:

1. Make sure goose legs are completely dry. Salt them liberally and set aside, skin side up. Allow the legs to come to room temperature and allow the salt to work its way into the skin. Prick the skin all over with a sharp knife being careful not to prick the meat. This gives the fat a place to render out of and baste the skin, making it crispy and delicious!

2. Put the legs in a small casserole dish. The dish should be just barely big enough to fit the legs in a single layer. Pour a thin layer of fat into the bottom of the dish. If the legs are skinny, add more fat than if the legs have a nice layer of fat on them, up to about a 1/4 inch up the side of the dish.

3. Put the dish in the oven and turn up to 300 degrees. Do not preheat the oven.

4. Cook goose legs at least 90 minutes. It will probably take at least 2-3 hours. For a larger or older goose, it could take 4 hours. Start checking in on them after about 90 minutes. It should be partly submerged in fat and the skin should be getting crispy.

5. Once the skin starts to get crispy, turn the oven up to 375 degrees. Cook at this temperature for 15 minutes or until the skin gets a nice golden-brown color on top. Remove from oven and let cool for 10-15 minutes before eating.

Goose legs slow cooked in a nice layer of fat and salt…mmm!

You can enjoy these legs as is or go the extra mile and turn them into some authentic goose carnitas, a BBQ pulled goose sandwich, or as part of a rich, tomatoey Italian dish.

You can also toss them in your favorite wing sauce and turn them into a Buffalo-style goose leg dish for snacking on while watching your favorite sports team!

With all those yummy options, you're probably kicking yourself that you've been wasting your goose and duck legs all this time!

It's important to remember that these legs do need to be cooked for quite some time. While not as tough as pheasant's legs, they are still quite tough and need extra cooking time to break down and tenderize.

Please Don't Feed the Vultures

Another common trope from hunters who regularly discard the carcass after breasting out the bird is that the remaining carcass and meat won't be going to waste. It will be feeding the vultures, crows, and other scavengers that will feast on the body once they're finished with it.

That's what road kill is for, my friends.

Whether you merely breast out the bird or actually take the time to pluck it and then roast it whole or in parts, you can still make use of your goose carcass and some of the giblets.

You can even use the feet as well.

One of the best ways to make use of every bit of the bird is by making a stock or bone broth out of it. You can then use your stock to make a range of other dishes: soup, pasta, risotto, polenta, sauces, and more. Like many other goose dishes, the process isn't hard, it just takes a little bit of time.

What's nice is that it's the same process for any type of bird: chicken, pheasant, duck, turkey, grouse…whatever. You can use this same recipe and just change out the type of bird you use with it. You now have a constant supply of delicious, nutritious, homemade stocks to flavor all sorts of food with.

Goose Stock

- 2 - 3 wild goose carcasses plus giblets like heart, neck, wing tips, and feet if possible
- Olive oil
- 1 whole onion, quartered, skin on
- 2 celery stalks, quartered
- 2 carrots, quartered
- Handful of parsley
- 3 bay leaves
- 3 garlic cloves
- Salt
- 1 tbsp. black peppercorns
- Large stock pot

Instructions:

1. If you're using carcasses from geese that have already been roasted, throw those in a stock pot with all other ingredients.

2. If you're using carcasses from birds that you just breasted out but didn't roast, chop them up, toss them in olive oil, and spread out in a roasting pan with other duck bits, bar the feet. Roast in an oven at 400 degrees around 30 - 45 minutes or until well browned.

3. If you have duck feet, chop them with a cleaver or butcher's knife to break the skin and expose the bones. The feet have tons of collagen which will make a richer, fuller bodied stock. Put the feet into the stock pot.

4. When duck carcasses are browned, place them in the stock pot as well with all additional veggies, salt to taste, and pepper. Cover with cold water at least 2-3 inches above carcasses.

5. Cover pot with a lid and bring to a boil. As soon as stock comes to boil, slightly uncover pot leaving lid halfway on and lower heat to a gentle simmer.

6. Allow to gently simmer 3-4 hours, checking on stock every hour to make sure it's not reducing too quickly. Stock should reduce by at least half, but you can reduce it more for even more concentrated flavors depending on how you want to use your stock in the future.

7. When stock is reduced, strain your stock. Put a colander over a large plastic container. Line the colander with paper towel. Ladle or pour stock into the colander to strain.

8. From there, you can refrigerate it for up to two weeks or portion into jars or freezer bags and freeze for future use. If freezing, be sure to leave at least 1 1/2 inches from the top of the jar or the bag to allow for expansion or else the jars will crack.

Using stocks is an excellent way to add additional flavor to any dish. When boiling rice, quinoa, or other grains, <u>always</u> use stock instead of water to impart a richer, deeper flavor to your food.

Use lighter stocks like chicken or upland bird stock for lighter grains like white rice or quinoa. Use darker stocks like duck and goose stock for heavier, denser grains like wild rice or barley.

These rich, concentrated stocks will also make a great base for many varieties of soup. You can make broth style soups like pho or wonton soup, or use it to flavor a hearty goose or beef stew with vegetables.

Stock is also required for any variety of pan gravies or sauces. Using the stock made from the carcass of the very animal you're serving up to make a rich gravy is the perfect complement to any meal.

If you make a lighter concentration of the broth, you can even use it as satisfying drink to put in a thermos and take with you to the blind. It will warm your bones as you're waiting in the cold for the birds to fly and provide plenty of nourishment as well.

Exclusively Goose: More Recipes

Curing and smoking goose are two methods that are particularly well-suited to goose. Brining and aging are also steps that are optional with other kinds of game but that become practically mandatory for the more fussy game that is goose.

I also showed you how to better use up the whole bird instead of wasting tons of usable parts by just breasting it out and discarding the rest.

I wanted to leave you with at least a few ideas for more conventional goose recipes. These are recipes that most people are already familiar with but that can be adapted to using wild goose breast or legs.

I'm hoping to at least inspire you and get your creative juices flowing. It's easy to get stuck in a rut with wild game by using the same recipes over and over again. Using some of the techniques discussed earlier in this chapter, here are a few more goose recipes you can try at home. Modify as needed to adapt to using wild goose breast instead of beef in most cases.

- Wild goose stroganoff
- Goose kabobs
- Chicken fried goose
- Goose Schnitzel
- Goose pot stickers
- Goose barbacoa
- Goose stew
- Goose gumbo
- Goose taquitos
- Braised goose ragu
- Goose egg rolls
- Goose stir fry

Between the recipes listed above plus all the various cooking and prepping techniques I've given you throughout the cook, hopefully you'll no longer look at cooking goose as such a daunting task. All it takes is three or four solid recipes to take you from a goose cooking noob to a legendary waterfowl

222 | Haley Heathman

cook able to impress, or even deceive, your friends with your expertly prepared meals.

You'll feel much better about yourself now that you know how to use up the whole bird to its full potential. When we know better, we do better. Now you know a lot more about how to hunt better, clean your game faster, and cook better.

With this knowledge, I hope you're able to go forth and continue being good ambassadors for the hunting world while maximizing your own success and enjoyment of the sport!

APPENDIX

Lists on Lists on Lists

There's nothing worse than getting into the field and realizing you left a crucial piece of hunting gear behind. Whether it was a backup call for your ducks or your game bags for your big game, nothing can ruin a hunt faster than not being adequately prepared.

Fortunately for you, I had a team of experts come up with the ultimate to-do list/gear list to make sure you're totally prepared in the days leading up to and for the duration of your hunt. Make a copy of these lists and be sure to check all the boxes that apply as you prepare for your big outing. The more organized you are in advance, the more successful you'll be in the field.

These checklists correspond to each of the different sections in this book. I've even included a checklist for you bow hunters out there as well.

These checklists are going to be massively helpful to the rookie hunters out there who sometimes don't even know what it is they're missing. These checklists are a compilation based on decades of experience from hunters who've already been there and forgotten that! In other words, you get to learn from others' mistakes so you don't accidentally go out on a hunt unprepared.

I hope you find these useful. Happy hunting!

Rifle Hunting Overview

Multiple pack options are important if you're heading out on a week-long hunt. Based upon the type of hunting, their contents are going to change daily.

If you're shooting antelope at long range, you're certainly not going to bother with face paint or a stove and freeze-dried meal; it's better to travel fast and light with the bare minimum to get the job done.

If you're heading out into the thick brush or heavy timber, coffee and energy drink sachets, a stove, and a freeze-dried meal are on board. The ideal pack for this situation is, of course, much larger and may incorporate a frame for packing out game.

An impromptu overnight camp might be on the cards so being prepared for this is important. Satellite messengers and GPS have become valuable tools. Letting friends and family know you're not coming home that night but are safe and sound is good etiquette and will create peace of mind for all.

It is always wise to calibrate your GPS prior to heading out on the trail. Many people get turned around when the arrow on the screen seems to be pointing in a different direction to their heading. Calibration doesn't take long and is a very simple process that is well worth doing. A topographic map and a simple compass are a great backup too.

In wet, muddy, or snowy conditions, duct tape covering the muzzle of your barrel can save you from a dangerous situation. Clogged barrel bores can cause excessive pressures.

Rifle Checklist

Initial Preparation

- Hunting regulations
- Dates of hunt: Best weather and moon phase days—plan daily locations accordingly
- Scouting and land ownership check
- Region and zone/district check
- Sunrise/sunset tables
- Hunting license
- Tags
- Verify rifle sight legality
- Let someone know where you're going and when you'll be back
- Clothes washed in scent free detergent
- Zero rifle check

Guns and Ammunition

- Rifle in case or horse scabbard
- Correct ammunition
- Rifle magazines if necessary
- Drop tables for rifle—correct ammunition
- Extra ammunition
- Monopod/bipod/tripod/shooting sticks
- Spotting scope and tripod/car window mount.
- Gun cleaning kit

Pack—Variety Taken

- Range finder
- Binoculars
- Satellite Messenger
- GPS
- Spare batteries
- Head Light
- Multi tool
- Wind indicator powder
- Bear spray
- Calls
- Knives
- Pen
- Wipes
- Light stick (hang by blood)
- Tape for tags and muzzle
- Game bags
- Plastic bags
- Survey tape or trail markers
- Latex gloves
- Medical kit
- Moleskin for blisters
- Pain killers
- Lip balm
- Toilet paper
- Space blanket
- Water purification (tablets/straw)
- Whistle & signal mirror
- Hydration bag for packs
- Chemical hand and feet warmers
- Lighter
- Fire starter

- Snacks
- Energy drink

As-needed Items

- Water bottle
- Stove
- Propane
- Lighter
- Freeze-dried meal
- Spoon
- Coffee
- Thermos
- Cup
- Scent control products
- Scents
- Rattlers
- Deer drag
- Tarpaulin
- Rope
- Carabiner
- Belay device
- Webbing strap
- Face paint
- Flashlight
- Compass
- Inflatable seat
- Topography map
- Charger chords
- Small towel
- Thermos
- Radios (depending on legality)
- Spare wind indicator powder

Clothing

- Blaze orange hat and vest
- Outer shell as required
- Layers as necessary
- Extra socks
- Two pairs of boots
- Gloves
- Balaclava/face mask
- Beanie/hat
- Sunglasses/shooting glasses
- Ear plugs

Post Hunt

- Call/text safe
- Cooler and ice
- Extra water and food

Bow Hunting Overview

Bow hunting can be one of the most rewarding or frustrating pastimes. Having that bull elk bugling within sixty yards in heavy timber sure is an amazing sight to behold, but if that's as close he comes...damn, that's infuriating!

Besides the usual necessary bow hunting equipment being on the list, there are quite a few other things to consider that are different to a rifle hunt in general season.

Here are a couple:

Weather

Sometimes it can be hot in early season—too hot. Be sure you're going to be hunting in conditions which will allow you to harvest and field dress your quarry ethically.

Check if your bow sight is legal where you are hunting

You may have a great single pin sight with a slight magnification and even an illuminated reticle. Even though you've practiced long and hard with this and are dialed in, this type of set-up might be illegal for the out-of-state hunting trip you've planned.

You may want to carry a hand gun or other firearm depending on your location and time in the field, just make sure to check legalities.

Be safe out there

Sometimes bow season coincides with some firearm seasons. For instance, in Montana, the archery season for deer and elk can start around the first part of September and continues through to the middle of October.

Meanwhile, fall bear season starts September 15 and runs through to the end of November. This means there are hunters out in the woods with firearms during deer and elk archery season. It might be wise to carry some blaze orange with you for the hike.

If you're going on a multi-day bow hunt, a spare release for your compound bow is an absolute must for your pack. There is nothing worse than losing your release without one to spare.

It's also advantageous to have a couple old arrows in your quiver. If you're doing it right, you shouldn't need six of your best arrows to take down your game. These can also be useful on the hike back to camp in case you come across a nice fat squirrel, rabbit, or grouse for the pot.

Bow Hunt Checklist

Initial Preparation

- Hunting regulations
- Dates of hunt: Best weather and moon phase days—plan daily locations accordingly
- Scouting and land ownership check
- Region and zone/district check
- Sunrise/sunset tables
- Hunting license
- Tags
- Verify pin distances on compound bow sight—bow sight legality
- Check/wax strings
- Let someone know where you're going and when you'll be back
- Clothes washed in scent free detergent

Archery Equipment

- Bow—stored in case or in horse pack bow scabbard
- Check arrows
- Quiver
- Glove and stringer (traditional bow)
- Release for compound bow
- Broadheads
- Old arrows with small game heads
- Arm guard

Clothing

- Balaclava/face mask
- Outer shell gear as necessary
- Layers as necessary
- Extra socks
- Two pairs of boots

Packs—Variety Taken

- Range finder
- Binoculars
- Knives
- Hydration bags for packs
- Satellite messenger
- GPS
- Spare batteries
- Head light
- Multi tool
- Bear spray
- Medical kit
- Lip balm
- Moleskin for blisters
- Pain killers
- Wipes
- Water purification (tablets/life straw)
- Whistle & signal mirror
- Toilet paper
- Space blanket
- Lighter
- Fire starter
- Snacks
- Pen
- Calls
- Light stick (hang by blood)

- Survey tape or trail markers
- Latex gloves
- Wind indicator powder
- Tape for tags
- Game bags
- Face paint

As-needed Items

- Blind and blind chair
- Bow hanger for blind
- Screw in hangers
- Stove
- Propane
- Freeze-dried meal
- Spoon
- Coffee
- Belay tool
- Rope
- Carabiner
- Webbing strap
- Tarp
- Plastic bags
- Flashlight
- Hand warmers
- Compass
- Spare wind indicator powder
- Gun cleaning kit
- Handgun and ammunition, if required
- Spare release
- Blaze orange hat and vest
- Scent control products
- Scents
- Rattlers
- Gloves

- Beanie
- Energy drink
- Inflatable seat
- Deer drag
- Small towel
- Thermos
- Cup
- Topography map
- Charger cords
- Radios, depending on legality

Post Hunt

- Call/text safe
- Cooler and ice
- Extra water and food

Upland Bird Overview

Upland bird is many people's favorite style of hunting. Not only can one get to hunt with good friends in an easy chatting scenario, but it's a great way to spend time with man's best friend—a hunting dog!

The birds are plentiful after a day's hunt, especially if you go on a guided hunt in a stocked field. They'll provide good eating for several weeks after your hunt!

Upland bird (besides turkey hunting) is a relatively easy pack for a day or two excursion. In most situations, you can drive up to the hunting location and even through an area (if permitted) to save yourself from extended walks. This is great if you have someone joining you who might have mobility issues. Relocate your transport a little to hunt a new section. Things get a little more interesting in mountainous locations for grouse or rough terrain for wild pheasant in grizzly country.

The below checklist covers all of the aforementioned scenarios. Turkey is included in this section as Upland packs and vests tend to work just as great for them as they do for chasing Hungarian partridge, chukkars, grouse, pheasant and quail.

Upland Bird Checklist

Initial Preparation

- Upland bird hunting regulations
- Sunrise and sunset hunt hours
- Dates of hunt: Weather and moon phase—best days
- Scouting and land ownership check
- Hunting license

Clothing

- Boots and gaiters
- Blaze orange
- Eyewear
- Earplugs
- Hat
- Packable rain jacket
- Upland brush pants
- Layers as necessary
- Extra socks
- Gloves

Pack

- Upland bird pack/vest
- Lip balm
- Moleskin for blisters
- Multi tool
- Head lamp
- Knife
- Water bladder (for human consumption)
- Snacks
- Toilet paper
- Whistle and signal mirror
- Lanyard

Pre-hunt

- Tell someone where you're going and when you'll be back
- Changing mat

Guns and Ammunition

- Shotgun
- Correct ammunition for game
- Shotgun cleaning kit
- Correct chokes and choke wrench

Dog

- Medical kit
- Pliers for quills and splinters (multi-tool check)
- Dog GPS collars and chargers
- Dog tone collar and charger
- Collapsible dog bowl
- Dog whistle
- Dog water bottles
- Dog food

Post Hunt

- Call/text safe
- Towels for both dog and you
- Extra change of clothes
- Cooler/ice
- Extra water

As-needed Items

- GPS
- Satellite messenger
- Spare batteries
- Bear spray
- Bug spray
- Sunscreen
- Shotgun shell bag
- Stove
- Propane
- Lighter
- Freeze-dried meal
- Spoon
- Coffee
- Whistle and signal mirror
- Extra water bottle

Blind (For Turkey)

- Blind bag
- Cutters for blind material
- Twine for blind material
- Gloves
- Hat/beanie/balaclava/mask
- Calls—owl, box, mouth
- Binoculars
- Chemical warmers for hands and feet
- Face paint
- Inflatable seat pillow
- Decoys

Waterfowl Overview

Waterfowl hunting can be a solo or group affair done from a boat, a lay-out blind in a field, or stalking flooded timber. The list below encompasses all of the items that may be necessary for any of the above situations and then some.

You may not have to take everything listed into the field, but all of the listed items should be available in your truck or on the go-to shelf during duck season. For instance, sunscreen might be on the list but won't be useful on a snowy November morning.

First and foremost, read the latest hunting regulations for the region and local area you are intending to hunt. Bag and possession limits change. Your daily bag limit in your chosen area might be seven ducks (with only two hen Mallards in that seven), but your possession limit might be three daily limits.

If you limit out each day in the first three days of your week-long duck hunting trip (nicely done!) and haven't eaten any at camp, then technically you can't shoot any more without being illegally over the possession limit.

Sunrise and sunset tables will vary as well. Check and verify the tables for your chosen zone. Authorized shooting hours could begin a half hour before sunrise and end at sunset each day of the hunting season unless otherwise stated in the regulations.

Waterfowl Checklist

Initial Preparation

- Migratory bird hunting regulations
- Scouting and land ownership check
- Dates of hunt: Weather and moon phase what are the best days—plan locations for set up each day accordingly
- Waterfowl ID guide
- Hunting license
- Federal Migratory Bird Stamp
- Sunrise/sunset tables

Clothing

- Waders
- Wading boots
- Outer weatherproof shell jacket and pants
- Layers as necessary
- Two extra pairs of socks

Pre-hunt

- Tell someone where you're going and when you'll be back
- Changing mat
- Head lamp

Guns and Ammunition

- Shotgun in floating case
- Gun cleaning kit
- Non-toxic ammunition for both ducks and geese (e.g. steel or tungsten)
- Chokes and choke wrench

Blind

- Blind bag
- Cutters for blind material
- Twine for blind material
- Blind chair/mud or slough seat/bucket with seat lid
- Blind gloves
- Warm hat
- Eyewear
- Earplugs
- Duck and goose calls—lanyard
- Binoculars
- Chemical warmers for hands and feet
- Medical kit
- Bug spray
- Lip balm
- Moleskin for blisters
- Toilet paper
- Sunscreen
- Face paint
- Snacks
- Water
- Thermos
- Cups
- Propane heater and fuel
- Flashlight
- Knife
- Stove and fuel
- Lighter

- Freeze-dried Meal
- Spoon
- Coffee
- Whistle and signal mirror

- Satellite messenger
- Spare batteries
- Bear spray
- PFD (personal floatation device)
- Kayak and paddle
- Two pairs of boots

Decoys

- Waterproof decoy Gloves
- Decoys—floating/field/motorized (batteries charged and chargers packed)
- Decoy bag
- Texas rigs and spares

Dog

- Medical kit
- Dog warmer mat
- Dog tone collar and charger
- Dog bowl
- Dog blind
- Dog vest
- Dog whistle
- Dog food & water

Post Hunt

- Call/text safe
- Towels for both dog and you
- Extra change of clothes
- Cooler/ice

As-needed Items

- Wader repair kit
- Multi tool
- GPS

ABOUT THE AUTHOR

Haley Heathman developed her taste for fine cuisine traveling the globe and working side by side with some of the world's most accomplished chefs. A lover of hunting and wild game, she uses her culinary skills to elevate wild game from mere survival gruel to tasty, refined meals that even non-hunters will enjoy. She lives in Florida with her family.

www.ingramcontent.com/pod-product-compliance
Lightning Source LLC
LaVergne TN
LVHW091039160125
801465LV00019B/93